Splash Hit!

WATERHOUSE

GIANTS

Splash Hit!

PACIFIC BELL PARK and the SAN FRANCISCO GIANTS

JOAN WALSH *and* C. W. NEVIUS

CHRONICLE BOOKS
SAN FRANCISCO

IN ASSOCIATION WITH
AMY RENNERT BOOKS

Edited by Rick Clogher

ACKNOWLEDGMENTS

A Giant thank you to: Roberta Achtenberg, Mario Alioto, Jay Bryon, Kevin Casey, Orlando Cepeda, Jorge Costa, Nancy Donati, Sandy Eeds, John Elford, Bertha Fajardo, Alfonso Felder, Debbie Greiff, Dave Hatheway, Bill Hedge, Stuart Horwitz, Maria Jacinto, Aaron Kenedi, Brad Klung, Mike Krukow, Duane Kuiper, Scott MacVicar, Dr. Math, Rebecca Miles, John Miller, Jon Miller, Jim Moorehead, Tom Morgan, Mary Nevius, Carrie Plummer, Jim Rennert, Blake Rhodes, Ted Robinson, Bob Rose, Susan Rutherford, Bill Schlough, Lon Simmons, Kevin Skillings, Staci Slaughter, Nora Walsh-DeVries, Paul Wilner, and Kristen Zaremba. A standing ovation for the four people who formed an error-free infield: Shirley Casabat, Shana Daum, Missy Mikulecky, and Ilene Snider. And, finally, thanks to all of the writers and photographers and to the San Francisco Giants, who went to bat for us.

Library of Congress Cataloging-in-Publication Data available.

Hardcover ISBN: 0-8118-3175-2   Paperback ISBN: 0-8118-3203-1

CREDITS

Associated Press, pages 29, 35. *Peter DaSilva,* page 92. *Beth Hansen,* pages 93, 115 top and bottom right. *HOK Sport,* endpapers, page 51. © *Andy Jurinko, courtesy Bill Goff, Inc.,* page 20 middle and bottom [contact: www.goodsportsart.com]. *Andy Kuno,* pages 2–3; 15; 19; 64–65; 65 bottom; 68; 69; 71; 72; 75; 76–77; 78; 79; 80 top left and right, bottom left; 81; 86; 90–91; 116–117; 123; 124; 127; 139. *Mike Lachenmyer,* pages 1, 33, 38. *John G. Mabanglo/Agence France-Pressé Photo,* page 131 middle left, center, and right. *Brad Mangin,* pages 41, 62, 66, 83, 88, 89, 94, 97, 98–99, 100 bottom right, 103, 104–105, 114, 129, 132, 134, 135 [contact: brad@manginphotography.com]. *Colin McRae,* pages 16; 21 bottom right; 56 top and bottom left, bottom right; 65 top; 100 bottom left; 107; 108 top left; 120 [contact: colin@mcraephoto.com, 415-863-0119]. *Missy Mikulecky,* pages 26 left top to bottom, 28, 31 bottom right, 111, 128, 131 top. *Mitchell Photographics Plus,* pages 4–5, 8–9, 12–13, 22–23, 58–59, 73, 85, 118, 121, 136–137 [contact: 818-224-4649, www.aerialphotoart.com]. *Heidi Montoya,* page 115 bottom left. *Dennis Morris Photography,* pages 42–43 [contact: 888-528-9714]. *National Baseball Hall of Fame,* page 26 right. *Mark Richards,* pages 10–11, 36–37, 53, 57, 60, 61, 106–107, 108 top right, bottom, 138 [contact: 415-389-8253, www.markrichards.com]. *Eric Risberg/Associated Press,* pages 46–47, 55 [contact: erisberg@ap.org]. *Keith Rosenthal (artist in residence, Pacific Bell Park Collection),* pages 40, 45, 48, 119. *San Francisco Giants Archive,* pages 21 left, 25, 30, 31 top and bottom left, 32, 34. *Martha Jane Stanton,* pages 6–7, 21 top right, 56 top right, 70, 74, 80 bottom right, 84, 87, 100 top, 113, 130, 131 bottom left and right, 133, 140.

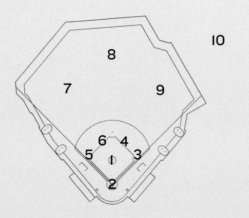

Book and cover design by Benjamin Shaykin
Photo editor: Louise Kollenbaum
Typeset in Miller, Knockout, Ziggurat, and Freehand 521

Distributed in Canada by Raincoast Books
9050 Shaughnessy Street, Vancouver, British Columbia V6P 6E5

Chronicle Books LLC
85 Second Street, San Francisco, California 94105

www.chroniclebooks.com

Starting Lineup

THE MIRACLE AT CHINA BASIN

by Peter Magowan and Larry Baer

IT WAS HALF AN HOUR before game time—the first game to be played at the new park—and we stood on the balcony overlooking Second and King Streets and watched it all come together. Down below a gathering of fans pressed closer, on foot, on bicycles, in cars, and on buses, trains, and ferries. Fans from the North Bay, East Bay, South Bay, and the City—all with one destination. Above the street, we hosted a gathering of friends and colleagues— workers, business and neighborhood leaders, consultants, politicians, volunteers, and other believers who had shared a dream with us and had seen that vision take shape in a brick-and-steel jewel beyond our expectations. Pacific Bell Park, a ballpark that some were already calling the city's newest landmark.

But we didn't set out to build a landmark.

We wanted simply to keep the game we loved and the team we loved from leaving the city we loved. That was what we faced in 1992: a harsh reality.

By the end of the '92 season, the Giants had been put on the block, and baseball in San Francisco seemed doomed. Local fans at the last home game begged the Giants to stay. But newspaper headlines shouted that the deal had been done, and the media had all but closed the book on the team's

West Coast story. Almost everyone in the Bay Area believed the Giants to be on their way to Florida.

Almost everyone.

Call us deluded or driven, but we refused to believe. We came from different backgrounds, different coasts, but we had a common passion—the Giants. We had to keep the team from leaving.

Baseball gets to you like that. You cannot grow up in this country without being conscious of the national pastime. It is the most fundamentally American sport, and it fills our lives in just those moments when we can savor it: when children are not in school, when families spend more time together. It stretches from the first grass of spring to the last leaves of autumn. In between, as has often been said, it is the background music of summer.

It's that legacy, that continuity, that experience that we couldn't live without, that we couldn't let San Francisco live without. Luckily, we had one other thing in common: a business instinct for taking risks and not giving up on what we truly believed in.

Our first step was to put together an alternate bid to block the agreement that would have moved the Giants to Tampa Bay. The odds were against us. Time was against us. So we began to do everything in

our power—and a few things we had never imagined, like cold-calling almost everyone we knew—and eventually we brought together a group of investors who put up the $100 million necessary to buy the team.

As a condition of the purchase, we promised Major League Baseball that we would move with all deliberate speed to build a state-of-the-art facility in our region, a new home for the Giants so that they could move out of Candlestick Park. Of course, we had absolutely no idea how we would accomplish this. But having averted the grim prospect of the team leaving the area, we began to dream. Not just of keeping baseball here, but of moving it downtown and showcasing it to the fullest.

We'd worry about the details later.

Over the next three years, two of those details became abundantly clear. First, that there was overwhelming support for moving the Giants into a downtown ballpark. Second, that there was equally overwhelming opposition to having the taxpayers bear the burden of such a ballpark.

Four times since 1987 voters in the region had rejected plans to build a taxpayer-funded home for the Giants. During those years, the region also suffered a devastating earthquake and a massive firestorm. The message from the community was, in essence, We have enough to worry about; the ballpark is your problem.

If we were to abide by our promise to Major League Baseball, we needed a new approach; we had to get the community to see the ballpark in a new light. And that meant one thing: private financing.

Glorious ballparks have been built in this era, but not without substantial—usually total—taxpayer funding. Private funding was a pipe dream. Sports finance experts told us no bank would ever lend us the money. Or that we'd never be able to carry the debt if they did. Fellow owners told us that we'd squander our resources on construction and have no money left to field a competitive team.

But we persevered. We believed that privately financed ballparks had never been done in our generation because they had never had a driving vision behind them. We felt we had that vision. We didn't set out to build a landmark. We simply wanted to build the best ballpark we could imagine. A place that captured the tradition of baseball and looked to its future. And a place that would give something back to the city for years to come.

We contacted the only architect we wanted to work with: Joe Spear of HOK Sport, the designer of Baltimore's Camden Yards, Cleveland's Jacobs Field, and Denver's Coors Field. After looking at our available sites, we took his advice and chose China Basin, a spot that he felt rivaled that of the Sydney Opera House for sheer beauty, with views and a panorama better than at any stadium or arena in North America.

We urged him to dream and to draw, to create something fitting for the site. What we envisioned was a ballpark more compelling, more distinctive than any other of recent memory.

Good ballparks are one-of-a-kind facilities. In this sense they differ from the arenas for other sports. Every football field, every basketball court, every hockey rink must have the same dimensions, and it is the sameness of the dimensions that in large part dictates the homogenous nature of the facilities.

Holding a 1992 headline that mistakenly reported the Giants' move to Florida, Executive Vice President Larry Baer and President Peter Magowan celebrate the first season at Pac Bell Park.

Baseball is different. Yes, the pitcher's mound must be sixty feet, six inches from home plate, and the bases must be ninety feet apart. But after that there are no hard-and-fast rules. Center field can be 387 feet away, as it was at Cincinnati's Crosley Field, or 483 feet, as at the Polo Grounds. Right center can be deeper than dead center. Walls can be as high as an architect desires or as low as the fans please. It's the game that allows the architect to make each ballpark unique. Sadly, not all architects are up to the challenge.

One has only to go to the various multi-purpose stadiums built in the 1960s and 1970s to see how utterly unimaginative ballparks can be. These concrete circles—with their artificial turf, symmetrical dimensions, and unvarying outfield walls—are virtual carbon copies of each other. A fan watching a game in one of these stadiums has no idea whether he is in Philadelphia, Pittsburgh, or Cincinnati.

Sit in Wrigley Field, however, and you get a unique baseball experience. The ivy on the brick outfield wall, the fans on the rooftops across the street—you can be only

in Chicago. Or one look at the Green Monster in left and the "jury box" in right center, and you know you must be in Boston's Fenway Park.

We wanted our park to evoke the feeling of the best of the old parks, with Wrigley and Fenway as our models. Both were urban ballparks, readily accessible by foot or public transportation. Both were charming constructs of brick and steel, not uninspired designs realized in functional concrete. Both were intimate, grass-field parks. Both had distinct features that let you know where you were.

And both emphasized our favorite baseball color—green. Green grass, green seats, green steel, green roof. A restful color to offset the white of the uniforms, the bases, and the baseball, and the red-brown of the brick and infield.

The best ballparks, though, are created not by an architect; they're created by a site imposing itself on the architect. It was the nearby presence of Boston's Landsdowne Street that gave rise to the Green Monster. Similarly, the outfield terrace at Crosley Field was not some gimmick

More recent newspaper headlines get the Giants' story right. Some ballparks, the Giants think, get baseball right, such as Fenway Park (middle) and Wrigley Field, shown in these lithographs by Andy Jurinko.

sketched in by an architect—it was the natural terrain of Cincinnati.

Joe Spear rose to the occasion. He let the singular nature of the China Basin site shine through all aspects of his plans: the location was hard by the water, so it celebrated San Francisco Bay; the ballpark would sit in a district of warehouses and pier buildings, so it showcased brick and steel and limestone; it would be part of a working neighborhood, so it featured street frontage matching that of its neighbors.

Once we had a true representation of our ballpark, we could approach fans and po-

tential sponsors to share our vision, our crusade—to put baseball into a glorious setting without public money. Much of the vision was unprecedented: seat licensing had never been tried before in baseball; sponsorship had never been attempted to the extent we planned. At every step of the way, people were eager to tell us it wouldn't work. But with the help of models and drawings, our message was different. It wasn't simply "Buy a charter seat" or "Give us your financial support." It was "Help us, and we can build *this* ballpark."

For any modern ballpark to be success-

ful, it must have the amenities of the great, new parks—wide concourses for better fan circulation, quality concession stands, luxury suites for the corporate community, excellent sound and video systems, modern retail stores and restaurants. These parks present the game at its best and create new fans. We had heard the complaints of the die-hards, that such luxuries bring out fair-weather fans and dilute the passion of the game. But here's the cold, hard fact we faced: a baseball stadium with a devoted core of fifteen thousand fans cannot survive. It is the absence of these amenities—and the inability to remodel an older facility to provide them—that has doomed so many of the best old ballparks: Sportsman's Park in St. Louis, Forbes Field in Pittsburgh, Shibe Park in Philadelphia, Tiger Stadium in Detroit, and even Fenway Park. The luxuries and conveniences that surround the game of baseball have to change over time, so that the game itself can endure.

Almost any team these days has to work to increase its current fan base and to develop fans for the future. For the Giants, those efforts included deciding just how large we would make Pacific Bell Park. The answer was, clearly, much smaller than Candlestick.

Gone are the days when cities would gladly build multipurpose stadiums with a capacity of 60,000 or more, only to see them sit far more than half empty for baseball. Stadiums with excess capacity have, in fact, been a key factor in many teams' economic problems. With so many available seats, there's little incentive for fans to buy tickets before the day of the game. For the team, that means a revenue stream that's hard to predict and harder to control—both bad signs for business.

Most viable ballparks today hover between 40,000 and 50,000 in capacity. Coors Field is one of the largest, at 49,000, and Jacobs Field is one of the smallest, at 42,000. Both are successful. We went even smaller and have no regrets. A few thousand extra seats would have made a drastic difference in Pac Bell. We could have erected multitiered stands in the outfield, but that would have obscured the views—a sacrilege in a setting as breathtaking as ours. And it would have meant less than ideal seats for those outfield fans.

Fans have figured into all our major decisions about the ballpark, particularly in the decisions that led to two of its signature features.

The first is the Portwalk. By law, we had to keep that area along the water open to the public. We could have made the outside wall of the park a blank facade, a clear signal that you weren't welcome if you weren't a paying customer. The legendary Connie Mack took a similar tack when he built a high wall in his Shibe Park, to prevent nearby townhouse residents from peeking in at games. Instead, we chose to build gated fences into the wall, so that people walking by outside *could* watch the game. Now, when someone asks what our cheapest location is, we answer, "It's free!"

The idea of the "knothole gang" goes back to the beginnings of baseball, but for today's fans it's a concept unique in the major leagues. For us, it's an opportunity to turn passersby into fans.

The second feature is the playground area above the left-field bleachers, the Fan Lot. In its planning stages, this section of the park stirred up controversy. Hard-core fans said we were cheapening the game with cuteness; our detractors said we were manipulating children by exposing them to corporate marketing.

In answer, we share one simple truth: of all the major sports, baseball is the only one that still asks children to attend, and it's the only one that is still affordable for a family. To expect young children to follow a three-hour game with the same rapt attention as an adult is unrealistic. To not cater to those families, those children, is to lose the next generation of fans. And those successive generations of fans are the lifeblood of baseball.

The slides and the miniature ballpark playground give parents a chance to keep their children engaged and entertained. And in years to come, we hope to see those same families sitting together in the stands, sharing a Giants game the way families have for 118 years.

You see, what happens on the field is ephemeral. A team's fortunes run hot and cold and hot again. The same player goes from goat to hero overnight, or in the course of a game. But what happens within the confines of the park is lasting. Mothers and sons, fathers and daughters, grandparents and grandchildren, friends and lovers bond together in ways that statistics can't measure.

We didn't set out to build a landmark; we set out to create a great urban gathering place—a place where people could share the experiences that make those bonds. To be able to offer that to people in a great setting with an undeniable future is the real achievement.

The ballpark has already gotten praise from fans and critics. We believe it will also pass the most difficult test—the test of time. We're certain that fifty years from now, it will still be beautiful and unique, and by then it will have proudly established what it is only just beginning to create: its own history and tradition, its own stories to be told and retold from one generation to the next.

That's what landmarks are about.

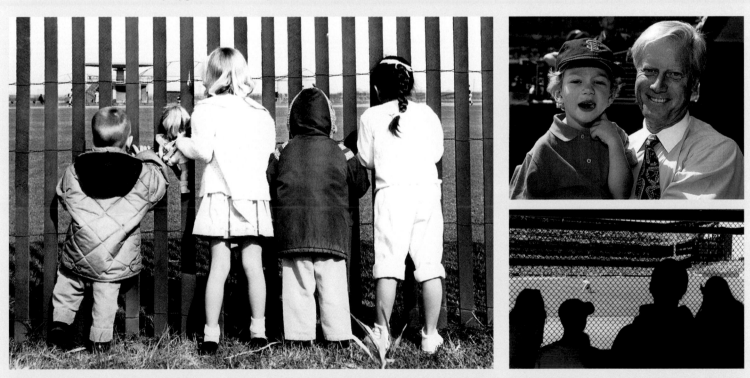

Baseball has been and always should be for the kids, like Peter Magowan's grandson, Alexander. That's why Pac Bell Park includes the Portwalk, to echo the days when kids could watch for free.

1 The Long Road Home

SOME SPORTS TEAMS HAVE A HISTORY. THE GIANTS EMBODY HISTORY. These days, franchises choose their team colors in marketing focus groups and pick a nickname based on how many fuzzy mascot dolls it will sell. The Giants, by contrast, are the original goods. They pitched two no-hitters, suited up seven future Hall of Famers, and won two postseason championships—all before 1900.

You want a long-standing rivalry? In the first-ever meeting between the two teams, the Giants defeated the Brooklyn Bridegrooms (later known as the Dodgers) six games to three in the 1889 championship (there was no official World Series until 1903). Game Four was marred by a huge rhubarb over an umpire's call. The teams haven't cared much for each other ever since.

Originally called the New York Gothams, the team was renamed in the 1885 pennant race, so the story goes, when manager Jim Mutrie, thrilled after an eleven-inning win over the Philadelphia Phillies, shouted, "My big fellows! My Giants! We are the people." Luckily, the New York Big Fellows didn't catch on, and it has been the Giants for more than a century.

The Giants were the first team to serve hot dogs (at the Polo Grounds in the early 1900s). They were the first to have a pitcher almost blown off the mound (Stu Miller in the 1961 All-Star Game). And they were the first—and hopefully the last—to have their home ballpark rocked by an earthquake during a World Series (1989).

About the only thing they haven't seemed to be able to do is stay in one place. From New York to San Francisco, from the Polo Grounds to Seals Stadium and Candlestick Park, this has been a

After seventy-five years in New York, the Giants relocated to San Francisco, becoming one of the first two major-league teams to move west of St. Louis. Crowds on Market Street welcomed the team, with players like Willie Mays and Hank Sauer, for its 1958 season.

The early Giants featured double trouble for opponents: the genius of manager John McGraw and the brilliance of Christy Mathewson, the team's most dominating pitcher. Above: Souvenirs from the McGraw era.

franchise in search of a home. Although the New York Giants were in the "Polo Grounds" for more than sixty years, the team actually played in four ballparks in three locations that bore that name. One structure burned to the ground in 1911, and the Giants shared the "new" Polo Grounds with the Yankees for ten seasons.

There was an undeniable magic to the most famous Polo Grounds, the quirky park that sat next to the cliffs of Coogan's Bluff. Its offbeat dimensions certainly gave it a character all its own—short fences in left and right that widened out to a cavernous center field that seemed to stretch on forever. But much of the magic came from the remarkable moments that took place in its confines, beginning with the unmatchable thirty-year run of John McGraw, who came to manage the Giants

"The short distances and asymmetrical shape of the Polo Grounds resulted in drives rebounding off of the left and right field walls like billiard shots." —Harvey Frommer, in his book *New York City Baseball*

in 1902. It was McGraw who saw the potential of young right-hander Christy Mathewson. Others wanted Mathewson to play first or shortstop, but McGraw installed him in the starting rotation, and for the next seventeen seasons Mathewson averaged almost twenty-two wins a year.

In the 1905 World Series "Matty" tossed three complete-game shutouts in six days to win the championship. With McGraw managing, the Giants were a force in the game for three decades, winning ten National League pennants and three World Series.

The Giants took their fourth Series title in 1933 under new manager Bill Terry. But after that, there was a long lull, broken only by the thunderous slugging of Mel Ott. In the late 1940s, team owner Horace Stoneham shook everyone out of their doldrums and kicked off the modern era of the Giants by hiring Leo Durocher, former manager of the despised Brooklyn Dodgers.

Four years after he took over, Durocher led the Giants to a playoff against . . . well, it had to be the Dodgers, didn't it? In the bottom of the ninth of the deciding game, trailing 4-1, the Giants scored once and put two runners aboard. With one out, Bobby Thomson slapped the second pitch he saw over the left-field wall. After that, there was a lot of yelling. You may have heard about it.

Durocher also had a young prospect he was pinning his hopes on—a center fielder who could hit, run, and throw. After a promising first season (he was named Rookie of the Year), the kid had to spend a couple of years in the army. But when he returned in 1954, Willie Mays was ready to reinvent the way the game was played—with his bat, with his legs, and with his glove. His over-the-shoulder catch in the 1954 World Series at the Polo Grounds is still on continuous replay wherever baseball highlights are being shown.

Above: Commemorative pins from Giants history. Opposite: Even though Mays says it's not his best, this is still the most famous catch—and arguably the most famous photo—in the history of baseball. Overleaf: Among the Giants' ten homes were Seals Stadium, the bathtub-shaped Polo Grounds, and Candlestick Park (open and closed).

But all was not well at Coogan's Bluff. Durocher left, the team faltered, and attendance slid disastrously. On August 19, 1957, Stoneham dropped the bombshell: he was moving the Giants to San Francisco. How, they asked in New York, could he do that to young baseball fans?

"I feel bad about the kids," Stoneham cracked, "but I haven't seen many of their fathers lately."

So the Giants headed west and settled into cozy Seals Stadium, where the Hamm's Beer sign endlessly filled and emptied a neon glass of beer behind home plate. To the surprise of nearly everyone, the Giants not only drew crowds on the West Coast, but they were contenders right from the start.

The established superstar was, of course, the incomparable Mays. General manager Chub Feeney would later admit that he had turned down a $1 million offer to trade the future Hall of Famer to St. Louis. Feeney joked that if he had made the deal, San Francisco fans would have heaved him into the Bay.

Along with transplanted New Yorkers, fans quickly had "homegrown" stars. Twenty-year-old Orlando Cepeda hit a home run on Opening Day and finished the 1958 season as Rookie of the Year. The next season, big Willie McCovey was called up for the stretch run, and in 1960 Juan Marichal, perhaps the greatest pitcher *never* to win the Cy Young Award, made his first appearance. That's three more Hall of Fame inductees right there.

Between 1958 and 1973, the Giants finished worse than third only three times. And in the unforgettable 1962 season, they took it all the way to Game Seven of the World Series against the New York Yankees. An entire book could be devoted to that final game alone. Let's just say that one interested fan called it the greatest Series game he had ever seen, and since that fan was Joe DiMaggio, you have to figure he knew what he was talking about.

As exciting as the Series was, it epitomized a Giants phenomenon. They were always tantalizingly close but never quite won it. After a nice run as contenders and a brief playoff appearance in 1971, another stretch of the doldrums set in. In 1972 the team fell below .500 for the first time, and attendance began to slip.

A sad, familiar pattern reemerged. By 1976, Horace Stoneham announced that he was moving the team again, this time to Toronto. It was the same old song, and Giants fans would hear it again and again. (Over the next twenty years, in fact, there would be reports of the team leaving for Tampa Bay, San Jose, Sacramento, and other points all over the map.) Only through the herculean efforts of Bob Lurie, who bought the team from Stoneham, was baseball saved in San Francisco.

Unfortunately, it wasn't very good baseball. The Giants sputtered in the late 1970s and early 1980s. There was grumbling about windy, cold Candlestick Park and the team foundered, eventually losing an even 100 games in 1985.

A black cloud seemed to hang over the 'Stick. The only hope was that someone would come along with the magic words to break the spell.

Officially a West Coast team in 1958, the Giants were one of the first two teams (with the Indians) to set up permanent training facilities in Arizona and have been there each spring since 1947.

And someone did. His name was Roger Craig, and the words were "Humm Baby."

Hired as manager late in the '85 season, Craig seemed to turn the Giants into a solid contender overnight. They reached the National League Championship Series in 1987, losing to St. Louis in a seven-game battle that will always be remembered for Jeffrey (Hac Man) Leonard's "one flap down" home-run trot. Two years later they brought the World Series to Candlestick Park for the second time.

But the 1989 World Series turned out to be most memorable for the game that wasn't played. Just before the start of Game Three, the 7.1 Loma Prieta earthquake struck. When the shaking stopped, the Candlestick crowd, still primed for a game, gave a hearty cheer. It was no laughing matter, however. After a ten-day delay, the Series resumed, but the joy had evaporated. The Oakland A's won in a four-game sweep.

FORM FOLLOWS FUNCTION

by George F. Will

BASEBALL HISTORIANS—that is a capacious category; all real baseball fans are steeped in the history of their sport, which now spans almost two centuries—can probably agree that the three most important developments in baseball since the Second World War were the breaking of the color barrier by Jackie Robinson, the coming of free agency for players, and the rediscovery of the delights of thoughtfully designed ballparks.

Note well the terminology. We are not talking about "stadiums" (or "stadia," as pedants would want us to say). We are talking about parks, with all that the welcoming word implies in the way of pleasant openness and playfulness.

The new wave of constructive construction began on the East Coast, by the harbor in Baltimore. But it is on the West Coast that the wave has reached what is—so far, and perhaps for a long time—its apogee in Pacific Bell Park.

It is now clear—it sometimes takes a while for common sense to dawn on humankind—that when God designed San Francisco's China Basin, He had in mind a setting for a diamond. Framed by the histrionic geography of America's loveliest city, there now is a work of art worthy of this frame.

But it is a functional work of art, a work that illustrates an old truism: form suited to function has a special beauty. Think of the old clipper ships that used to sail in and out of San Francisco Bay. (And while you are at it, think of the San Franciscan whose gracefulness earned him the sobriquet "the Yankee Clipper.") Those ships had a special elegance not because naval architects set out to achieve elegance, but because they set out to design vessels perfectly suited to their tasks. Pac Bell Park is a similarly happy marriage of form and function.

Again, it is a matter of common sense, but common sense that was lost sight of

for a generation or so, during which ghastly "dual-purpose" stadiums were built to accommodate both baseball and football, stadiums that served both sports very badly indeed. The function of a ballpark, properly executed, is to display, and by its design to add some spice to, the most observable of team games—players thinly dispersed across a broad green field.

The recipe for doing this is to have intimacy. This should be intimacy for more than 40,000 but fewer than 50,000 fans. And it should be intimacy achieved by good sight lines and small foul territory. The recipe is also to have an outfield configuration not produced by a giant cookie cutter but rather by real baseball minds—by

people who understand that angles and height variations of the outfield walls produce triples and other good things.

But why try to describe the recipe in words? The recipe has been fully realized at China Basin.

It has been well said that architecture is frozen music. The architecture of Pac Bell Park captures, in brick and steel, the tune that is at the top of every baseball fan's hit parade, "Take Me Out to the Ball Game." And Pac Bell is a splendid setting for the singing, eighty-one times a year, of our national anthem, the last eight words of which are, as every fan knows, ". . . and the home of the brave play ball."

George F. Will, a Pulitzer Prize–winning columnist and contributing editor to *Newsweek* magazine, is the author of eleven books, including two bestsellers on baseball, *Men at Work* and *Bunts*.

As had happened so often in the past, the Giants went from a brief high to a prolonged low. It seemed to be the curse of Candlestick that dragged the team down. The team would draw at the gate if it made the playoffs, but even a die-hard fan had a difficult time sitting through a Tuesday night game late in a losing season.

In 1992, even Lurie gave up. He announced that he was selling the team to a group in Tampa-St. Petersburg. The final game of the 1992 season was a farewell party. Fans held up signs that begged, "Please, stay," and the players came out of the dugout after the game to wave good-bye. It looked as if the Giants were exiting for good.

Enter, instead, a spark of hope, in the person of Peter Magowan, a Giants fan of such devotion that during the 1950s he used to listen to the games on a transistor radio at his boarding school in Massachusetts. A transplanted New Yorker and a member of the Giants board of directors, he began to put together a partnership group rather than see his team move cross-country a second time.

They scratched and clawed and with a little encouragement from Major League Baseball managed to acquire the team in late 1992. Then they announced the shocker: the team had signed Barry Bonds, simply the best player in the game.

If getting Bonds was unimaginable, signing Dusty Baker to manage was downright inspired. The team immediately got back on track: they won 103 games in 1993, Baker's first year; and in 1997, energized by two late-season miracle wins over the Dodgers, they made it to the playoffs.

The Giants lost that playoff series to the eventual World Champions, the Florida Marlins. A disappointment, but the Magowan group had bigger dreams.

Magowan and his partners set out to solve the foremost problem that had plagued the team since it moved west. Using an innovative plan, they put together the first privately financed ballpark in thirty-eight years. And it was a gem—Pac Bell Park.

That's why on April 11, 2000, when the players trotted onto that sparkling new field, into a ballpark packed with fans, it was the completion of a long circle. After all these years, the Giants were finally home.

2 *The Jewel of the Waterfront*

PACIFIC BELL PARK IS SPECIAL FOR THREE REASONS: LOCATION, LOCATION, and location. Rising from the shores of San Francisco Bay, this is the ballpark that has it all—stunning views, sunny weather, and its own sailing armada.

Pac Bell is a minor miracle on many levels. The famous wind off the Bay has been tamed, the surrounding neighborhood south of Market Street has been revitalized, and the taxpayers' purse has never been touched. The moment you walk into the park, with its classic old-timey feel, and see tankers drifting under the Bay Bridge, you can't imagine a ball yard that says "San Francisco" any better. And that's the irony.

For a long time, you see, it seemed the Giants' new home would be located anywhere but here. Alternatives ranged from a South Bay stadium (that idea got so serious that locals printed uniforms with *Santa Clara* across the chest) to a giant dome somewhere downtown.

There were proposals to put a Giants ballpark on the rail yard at Seventh and Townsend Streets and even a wild scheme that would have created an immense floating stadium tethered to the shore.

Some of the ideas, like the dome and the barge ballpark, died of disinterest and common sense. But four others proved serious enough to reach the ballot, where they were voted down by taxpayers.

Each election felt like a bitter setback at the time, but Pac Bell Park as we know it today would never have existed if any of those ballot measures had passed. As a longtime Giants fan joked on Opening Day of the new ballpark, "Thank God the Giants lost all those elections."

Where once there was only an empty lot and deserted warehouses, today stands Pac Bell Park, looking as if it's been there for decades, the highlight of the city's southern waterfront.

Actually, the 1989 plan, called Proposition P and promoted by then-mayor Art Agnos, looked like a sure thing. The ballpark would have been built on the same China Basin site, and even though the plan involved taxpayer financing, it appeared headed for a certain win in the November election. But on October 17, 1989—in what can *only* be described as an act of God—the Loma Prieta earthquake changed everything.

"Pac Bell Park is to Shea Stadium what San Francisco is to Newark."
—Kevin Kernan, *New York Post*

The terrible temblor hit the Bay Area minutes before Game Three of the Giants-A's World Series was set to begin at Candlestick Park. It toppled whole blocks and set off fires in San Francisco's Marina District, collapsed the Cypress Freeway in Oakland, and made a vote on a baseball stadium seem totally irrelevant. Although Proposition P lost at the polls, it may have been a blessing in disguise.

Backers of the Agnos plan insist that it would have resulted in a ball yard just as nice as Pac Bell Park, but there is reason to think that the 1989 design would not have had the same flavor. In 1992, the Sports Facilities Group of Hellmuth, Obata, and Kassabaum (HOK), one of the world's largest architectural design firms, sparked a renaissance in ballparks with its design of Baltimore's Camden Yards, a modern stadium with the feel of grand old parks like the Polo Grounds and Fenway Park. (Chicago's new Comiskey Park, HOK's first major-league design in 1991, was more symmetric.) "Until Camden, we didn't have the example," says Pat Gallagher, president of Giants Enterprises. "But when you saw it, the lightbulb had to go on. That was the way to do it."

Giants Managing General Partner Peter Magowan, a baseball traditionalist to the toes of his

Two workers bolt concrete risers in place in the View Level; ironworkers head to the day's next task; and these anchor pegs will hold the attached steel plate to a vertical facade of poured-in-place concrete.

FROM GREEKTOWN TO CHINA BASIN

by Nick Peters

AS A YOUNGSTER GROWING UP south of Market, my imagination ran rampant during the bustling war years. It was the early 1940s, and the Bay Bridge and booming port and commercial activity had revitalized downtown San Francisco.

But never in my wildest dreams could I envision a ballpark just a few blocks from where I lived. China Basin was an area of dilapidated warehouses and images of urban blight. Families had abandoned it for the suburbs, and winos walked its streets. Yet the rundown area was a magnet for a wide-eyed youngster because of the Southern Pacific train terminal at Third and Townsend.

The handsome Spanish-style station buzzed with activity. Sleek streamliners like the Daylight and the Lark would pull in from Los Angeles. Commuters would pour in from the Peninsula and walk up crowded Third Street to Market and to the office buildings of Montgomery Street, the city's financial hub.

Baseball wasn't part of the mix then, except perhaps when the Los Angeles Angels or the Hollywood Stars came to town to take on the San Francisco Seals in Pacific Coast League games at Seals Stadium, just a mile away at Sixteenth and Bryant. More often, though, I'd walk from our house—my grandfather's three-story Victorian at 42 Perry Street, near Third between Harrison and Bryant—to admire the powerful locomotives at the train station or to play childhood games in nearby South Park.

Major-league baseball was a far more distant dream. The Giants belonged to New York and always had. For more than half a century, there were no major-league teams closer to us than St. Louis.

In my little world, baseball meant attending sandlot games with my dad at Father Crowley Playground on Harrison Street. By the mid-1940s, Seals Stadium had lights,

so they would brighten the night and cut through the fog as I watched from my bedroom window.

I learned about baseball from old-timers who would visit Dad's grocery store and deli, the Olympia Importing Company, at Third and Folsom. This was the heart of Greektown, a two-block, immigrant-rich stretch from Harrison to Howard. The afternoons would be filled with re-creations of major-league games on radio or Don Klein's broadcasts of the Seals.

Gradually, baseball replaced trains and trolleys for me, and trips to Seals Stadium for exhibitions with major-league teams like the Giants, Browns, Indians, and Yankees became more frequent.

By the time I was a teenager in the 1950s, I was hooked. I spent weekends watching our beloved Seals. If I let the mind reel, I can smell the hops from the nearby brewery, the aroma from the bakery down the street, and the roasted peanuts. I can remember Al Lien and Elmer Singleton pitching; Joe

Brovia, Max West, Steve Bilko, and Joe Grace at the plate; and Roy Nicely and Leo Righetti scooping up grounders at short. Who needed major leaguers when we had the Seals and the Oaks?

The sadness we felt at the Seals' demise following the 1957 season turned to joy once the Giants arrived in 1958. This was a better brand of ball, but we didn't immediately realize the difference.

Watching the incomparable skills of Willie Mays soon defined the difference. Juan Marichal, Orlando Cepeda, Willie McCovey, and Mays epitomized what we had been missing. Forty years later, a dazzling ballpark by the Bay tells us also what we have been missing for decades.

Just as Seals Stadium became a model for minor-league ballparks, cozy and comfortable Pac Bell has set the standard for the new, fan-friendly big-league park. And, once again, San Francisco has proved it still is the City That Knows How.

A native San Franciscan and sportswriter for the *Sacramento Bee*, Nick Peters completed his fortieth year covering the Giants with the 2000 season. He has written four books on his favorite subject: *Giants Diary, Giants Almanac, The Miracle of Candlestick*, and *Giants Encyclopedia*.

February 28, 199

November 28, 199

December 8, 199

> ## "Making the water part of the game, that's where the magic is."
>
> —Joe Spear, ballpark architect, HOK Sport

The recipe is simple: take about 2,100 pilings, 66,000 cubic yards of concrete, 10,000 tons of rebar, 4,000 tons of structural steel, 650,000 bricks, 2,000 workers, roughly $320 million, and one inspired vision; mix together and stir vigorously for slightly more than 800 days.

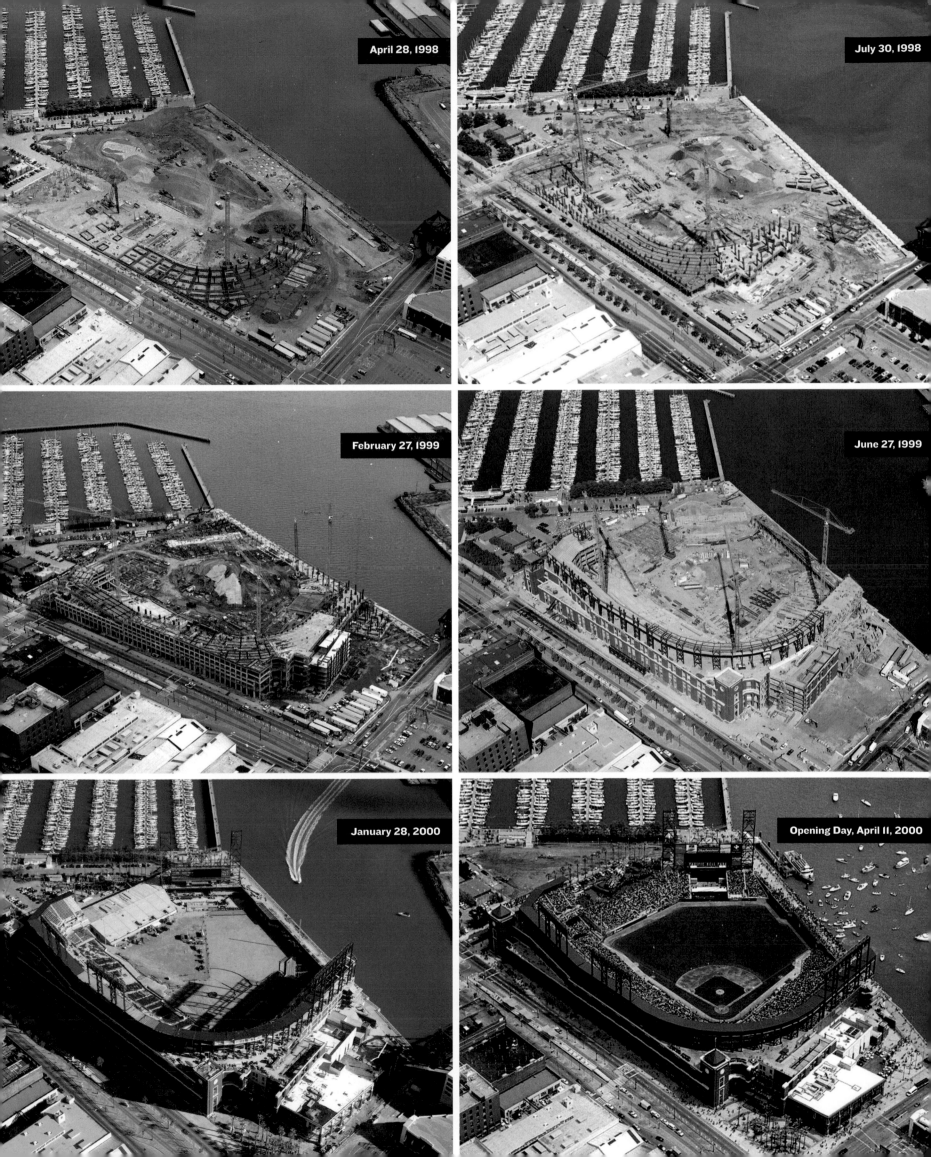

April 28, 1998

July 30, 1998

February 27, 1999

June 27, 1999

January 28, 2000

Opening Day, April 11, 2000

wing tips, certainly felt that way. When Magowan and the team announced the plans for the new yard, they made certain that it would be built in the new HOK mold—that is, it would be an intimate, baseball-friendly park with vintage touches such as a hand-operated scoreboard and a distinctive, irregularly shaped outfield wall.

The team insisted on HOK architect Joe Spear, whom Giants Executive Vice President Larry Baer calls "the Rembrandt of ballparks." Spear, who sketched the original plan for Camden Yards while doodling on a notepad, instantly recommended the waterfront spot as his firm's top pick for a site. He felt he could deliver what the Giants wanted: a home that Magowan and Baer envisioned as "Camden Yards meets Wrigley Field West."

Although the site, an abandoned, run-down slab of asphalt and concrete pushed up against the waters of China Basin, didn't look promising at first glance, it turned out to be an inspired choice.

"The Great Ballpark Building Battle is over. San Francisco won."

—David Lassen, sports columnist for the *Ventura County Star*

First, at only thirteen acres, bounded by the Bay to the south and east and by King and Third Streets to the north and west, the site had one of the smallest "footprints" Spear has ever worked with. Denver's Coors Field, another Spear project, takes up seventeen acres by comparison.

The cozy dimensions of the China Basin site created the most intimate park this side of Wrigley Field. Fans feel they are right on top of the action, and they are. In fact, the seats in the first row behind the screen are a dozen feet closer to home plate than the pitcher is. In addition, the presence of the boat channel made a short right-field "porch" a necessity. The result is Pac Bell's signature feature, the home run ball that splashes into what has been dubbed McCovey Cove.

There are other novel touches. San Franciscans love their history, and the ballpark site was literally created out of hunks of the city's past. When you visit Pac Bell Park, take a minute to walk to the other side of King Street (which runs parallel to the third-base line). The north side of the street roughly marks the edge of a bluff that sat above a sandy beach when San Francisco was a gold-rush boomtown. Over the years, timbers, bricks, and trash from construction were pitched over the side. Perhaps the biggest accumulation came after the famous 1906 earthquake and fire, when tons of debris was shoved off the hillside to make room for rebuilding. Gradually, a landfill built up, leveling the grade to the water but leaving mysterious bits of archeology behind. As Pac Bell Park took shape, timbers treated with creosote from piers and waterfront buildings turned up regularly. There were also smelly remnants of a coal-tar gasification plant that operated around the turn of the twentieth century.

All work, like the building of the concrete risers, proceeds assembly line style, beginning from behind first base and moving outward; home plate is installed early, since its position determines many of the park's measurements; and a worker helps to ready the right-field foul pole for installation. Overleaf: In January 2000, the Giants treat the construction workers and the media to a batting practice display in the nearly finished ballpark.

The fact is, we will probably never know all of what lies beneath the park. Although the construction firm of Huber, Hunt & Nichols/Kajima made a point to haul out any toxic substances that were discovered, the contractors barely scratched the surface of the site. There are two reasons for that, both of which contribute to Pac Bell's unique character.

First, as construction crews quickly confirmed, the water table is barely twelve to fourteen feet below what is now the green outfield grass. Whenever workers had to dig down more than ten feet, the hole quickly filled with salt water from the Bay. In fact, the facilities that are below field level at the ballpark, like the batting cages behind the dugouts, are actually lined with a waterproof seal, like huge bathtubs. If they spring a leak, Pac Bell will be the first major-league ballpark to have two full-sized swimming pools.

"Pac Bell Park has turned funky, activist, radical old San Francisco into something completely unexpected: a baseball town. The Giants have become as tough a ticket as the opera." —Tom Sabulis, *Atlanta Journal-Constitution*

Second, because the site is on landfill, it could not be trusted to be a stable base in earthquake country. What was needed was a deep, firm foundation. That was achieved by driving 2,100 reinforced concrete pilings down to the bedrock, in some cases as much as 100 feet below the surface. The ends of those pilings were then used as the foundation: contractors poured a honeycomb of concrete "gray beams" and tied it into the pilings, so the whole ballpark sits on the tips of long, strong rods that reach deep into the earth.

Oddly enough, those two factors—the shallow water table and the need to build on concrete pilings—helped create a benefit: the wind is not the problem that it was at Candlestick Park.

Think about this the next time you come to Pac Bell: at most modern ballparks, you enter a gate at ground level and then descend to field level. The inside of the stadium is scooped out of the earth to create a bowl, with seats built around the interior walls.

At Pac Bell, the *field* is at ground level (if it were much lower, you'd need scuba gear to steal second) and the three decks rise abruptly from there. This not only puts the fans closer to the field, but it also creates a steep and effective windbreak.

It's not the Real Thing, but it's the biggest Coke bottle replica around. Filled with soda, it could pour a case of Coke for each fan in Pac Bell Park, with plenty left over for the team.

Even as construction crews erected the upper decks, they noticed that the infamous summer breezes that made Candlestick such an ordeal were cut to almost nothing by the shear walls. If you don't believe it, go to the View Level on the first-base side some night and walk through the exit to the concourse on the outside of the stadium. Don't forget to hang onto your hat.

Finally, one thing all visitors notice about Pac Bell Park is the advertising. Not just the colossal soft-drink bottle in left field—a controversial project when it was proposed—but the signs that seem to crowd every available space.

There's a good reason for that, and it stems from what may be the most important feature of the park. Although it made them unpopular among their fellow Big League owners, who feared it might start a trend, the Giants built and financed the ballpark without any contribution from taxpayers. Magowan and his partners simply went to the bank, like any ordinary homeowner, and arranged for a $170 million mortgage. That made Pac Bell the first privately financed stadium since Dodger Stadium was built in 1962.

"From the upper deck of Pac Bell Park, fans could almost see 3Com Park at Candlestick Point, not more than three miles away. But it was like looking into another era, like looking at the back side of the moon."

—Carl Nolte, *San Francisco Chronicle*

The trade-off is that the team explores every possible revenue stream. From the extremely successful charter-seat plan to the naming rights, the Giants have worked to make this not only an attractive ballpark, but a financially successful one too.

Naturally, now that it is earning rave reviews, there will be those who will want to copy Pac Bell Park. No problem. It's a simple plan, really. Begin by constructing a full-size replica of San Francisco Bay. Everything else falls into place from there.

THE PARK WE DIDN'T BUILD

by Joe Spear

I REMEMBER when we got our first call from the new owners of the Giants, asking for our advice. They said the city had given them thirty days to state a preference for a site for a new ballpark. We immediately told them to go for China Basin.

Our firm had been involved in all the attempts by Bob Lurie to get a new stadium. So from previous studies we knew we could get a ballpark on that site. But we didn't know if it would be the kind of park that Peter Magowan and Larry Baer would want to build. I asked them to let me work up some plans, to show them how the seats would fit in, the luxury suites, basically how they could sell their product. But they weren't interested. They wanted to talk about the architecture. They asked, "Can you do a rendering of how a ferry would dock here? Or a rendering of the Portwalk and the King Street elevation? And the view from the upper deck looking to the Bay Bridge?"

I don't think we ever did talk about the number of suites. Throughout the process, Peter and Larry were committed to doing something that was bigger than the Giants.

It was really a no-pressure way to design a park. I'd just do sketches and fax them out to the Giants. There's one early rendering that shows the scoreboard in right field, along McCovey Cove. We had talked about it being there. But after we had structural engineers on the project and made some surveys, we came to find that that Portwalk is built on fill. We were concerned about the cost of having to build a structure out there capable of supporting a scoreboard—and concerned about the number of people who'd be able to see it well. We realized that by putting it where we ultimately did—nearly in dead center field—it wouldn't need a deep foundation and it would let more people in the grandstands see the video board better.

Actually, no one at HOK wanted the scoreboard to be anywhere in the outfield because it would block the Bay. But the geotechnical concerns tipped our hand.

At one point we even had an idea for a restaurant inside the scoreboard—it started out as a brew pub. But local restaurant people told us that if it wasn't convenient for taxis and cars to drop people at the door—especially on nongame days—it wouldn't survive. So we moved it to Third Street, and it became Restaurant Twenty-Four.

Another thing about the Portwalk: originally the outside wall was to be brick, like the King Street side. But at a review session, John Kriken, the architect from Skidmore, Owings & Merrill, asked, "Why the brick on the outside of the outfield wall?" He pointed out that pier buildings in San Francisco are either limestone or concrete or painted stucco—they're always light colored, which creates a beautiful reflection on the water. "I think you might want to change that brick," he said.

Someone from the Giants was at that session and worried what Peter would think. But I realized it was the right thing to do. The ballpark touches very different environments: the brick facades of King Street, the steel of the Lefty O'Doul Bridge, the water. And it's appropriate that it be different in those areas. We never looked back from that decision.

From the very first, we knew the China Basin site would be a challenge, but that it would be worth it. The site itself was pretty blighted, but you had the redeveloped China Basin building and the sailboat marina. And we knew the ballpark could be the missing link on that waterfront. With its view of the Bay and the Oakland and Berkeley hills, Treasure Island and the Bay Bridge—if Walt Disney were alive and designing a backdrop for baseball, he couldn't have done it better.

The most prolific major-league ballpark designer of the past decade, Joe Spear of HOK Sport has been the chief architect for Camden Yards, Coors Field, Jacobs Field, Comerica Park, Pacific Bell Park, and the soon-to-open Miller Park in Milwaukee.

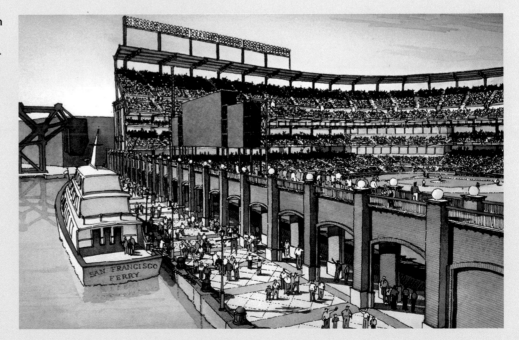

 **3** *And Finally, Opening Day*

THE WEATHER ITSELF SEEMS TO HERALD A NEW DAY FOR SAN FRANCISCO baseball, as Pacific Bell Park hosts its first game, a March 31 preseason contest against the Milwaukee Brewers. Two hours before game time, it's a balmy eighty degrees, as the sun shines down on a city transformed.

Normally desolate Third Street, which, fittingly, genuflects at Pac Bell and continues south to Candlestick Park, teems with shirtsleeved baseball fans. Around Townsend and King Streets, those on the already-crowded sidewalks have to make room for the many thousands who come by bus, train, and trolley. Mysteriously, miraculously, the long-predicted traffic gridlock never materializes as cars sail off freeway exits and head up and down Third and Fourth Streets with relative ease.

Just past Townsend, the procession on Third, those thousands of baseball pilgrims, gets a first glimpse of their new house of worship. The crowd seems to hush as the details of the park rise up before it: the twenty-four palm trees swaying above Willie Mays Plaza, the rings of light at the base of their trunks magically illuminating them, the statue of Mays standing rugged and graceful in front.

In bronze Mays is not yet thirty, and he's just hit a home run. His lithe, powerful body is at the end of a mighty swing; the bat is falling away, still cradled in his last three fingers, and he's looking skyward like all transcendents. Of all the marvelous new stadiums in major-league baseball, there's not another with so stunning an entrance. On the corner of Third and King this night there are fans with goose bumps, fans in tears.

The magic continues inside, as 40,930 newcomers get acquainted with their new baseball home. As you might expect, there are the inevitable first-day glitches and gripes about lines, but the

PACIFIC BELL.

307   13   1   15.00
sec   row   seat   price

PACIFIC BELL PARK
HOME OF THE SAN FRANCISCO GIANTS

OPENING DAY

SAN FRANCISCO GIANTS
INAUGURAL
YEAR   SF   2000

TUESDAY, APRIL 11, 2000 • 1:05 PM

GIANTS vs. Dodgers

View Reserved

8581241   MJS092-LKU2

307   13   1   15.00
sec   row   seat   price

overwhelming mood is elation—red-white-and-blue bunting always lifts the spirit. Never has a pre-season game felt so much like the postseason.

Midday had belonged to Willie Mays, with a grand ceremony to dedicate his statue and the Plaza. The likes of Bill Cosby, Giants great Bobby Thomson, and even Baseball Commissioner Bud Selig had come to welcome a new era of baseball to San Francisco and pay tribute to the living legend. Now, at game time, Mays turns the spotlight on the park and the team. He steps to the mound to

"The first day it opened I was standing behind home plate and I looked up and saw adults running down the aisles to get to their seats. It was like Christmas morning for 40,930 people."

—Mike Krukow, Giants broadcaster and former Giants pitcher

throw out the ceremonial first pitch—and with an impish glee fitting the occasion, deliberately tosses it to a lucky fan in the seats. He pulls a second ball from his pocket and rifles it in to his godson, left-fielder Barry Bonds. It's time to play ball.

The Giants win the exhibition, 8-3, and tally five extra-base hits in the process, as the Brewers seem to struggle with the new park's spacious center field. After the game, the bars and restaurants around the park throb with new life. Outfielder Ellis Burks even drops by MoMos at Second and King to have a drink and chat with fans. The regular season has not yet begun, but already one thing is clear: Pacific Bell Park has changed San Francisco, immediately, irrevocably, forever.

On April 11, the joy and pageantry of Opening Day top that of Opening Night. Kids skip school and grown-ups brazenly leave work to stroll to the new downtown ballpark. By 10:30 A.M. thousands of fans are waiting to pass through the electronic turnstiles for the park's official opening game against the hated Los Angeles Dodgers.

More than sixty boats—including kayaks and a canoe—dot the waters of McCovey Cove. Towering masts float majestically beyond the right-field wall. Even the umpires take a break from impartiality to marvel at the surroundings: "This is as pretty a park as there is in baseball," says Ed Montague, a San Francisco native who attended the Giants' opening games at Seals Stadium in 1958 and Candlestick in 1960 and whose father was the Giants scout who signed Willie Mays.

Three parachutists sail surreally toward the park, aiming for center field, but only two hit the mark (the third lands safely outside left field). The off-course chutist learns first what everyone will soon realize: the winds at Pac Bell will never torment fans the way they did at Candlestick, but they

The Say Hey Kid and the Splash Hit Kid: at the first exhibition game at Pac Bell Park, Willie Mays shares the moment after tossing the ceremonial *second* pitch to his godson, Barry Bonds. Mays threw the first ball to a lucky fan.

will tweak infielders and wreak havoc with pop flies, creating a singular brand of baseball apparent from the very first game.

At home plate, the cast of *Beach Blanket Babylon* sings "San Francisco." On the field, pageant participants unfurl a large American flag near the pitcher's mound. Then a second flag, larger, joins it in the shallow outfield. And then a third—a mammoth banner that almost covers the outfield from foul line to foul line.

Suddenly a formation of F/A-18 Navy Hornets buzzes the field, flying so low they seem to pass between the scoreboard light towers. Out in the Bay, the Coast Guard clears McCovey Cove, while a barge slowly chugs offshore. Jazz vocalist Bobby McFerrin comes to the plate and begins the national anthem, and when he reaches his crescendo the Hornets make their second pass. This time, a lone, trailing jet kicks in his afterburner and shoots straight up into the sky directly over the infield.

The Giants tip their hardhats to the construction effort by having workers do the final installation of the bases; *Beach Blanket Babylon*'s Val Diamond sports her new "cap"; the field gets a last watering; and Franciscan fathers Floyd Lotito and Dan Lackie bless the new ballpark, with Giants announcer Renel Brooks-Moon looking on. Overleaf: Hundreds of thousands of people will someday claim they were part of the Opening Day crowd; 40,930 will have the ticket to prove it.

TIME WARP *by Darryl Brock*

HEADING FOR MY FIRST Giants game of the 2000 season, I watch Pacific Bell Park loom ahead from my spot at the rail of the Alameda ferry—this watery approach is one of my favorite things about the new ballpark—and I can't help but carry in my mind an overlay of the past. I think back frequently to the first appearance of top-flight pros in San Francisco. Not in 1958, when the Giants moved into Seals Stadium. Rather, in 1869.

That was the year the Cincinnati Red Stockings—not the first players to be paid, certainly, but the first with salaried contracts as *ballplayers*—barnstormed the country, taking on all comers. Their journey over plains and mountains on the new transcontinental railroad eventually brought them to this gold-rush city.

Like me, those pioneer pros made the final leg of their trip to San Francisco by water, in their case by river steamer from Sacramento. And like the Giants, they played at a new site south of downtown. The Recreation Grounds at Twenty-fifth and Folsom was unique in its time. It was the only field on the West Coast to be completely fenced in, thus providing small boys with some of baseball's first knothole views. And like Pac Bell, it was built with private capital. There, on game days, horse-drawn shuttles arrived every fifteen minutes from downtown hotels (a fifty-cent fare included gate admission) and added to the already overflowing crowds.

On Twenty-sixth Street, a carriage entrance allowed the gentry from such plush neighborhoods as South Park and Rincon Hill to plant their vehicles around the outfield and look on in comfort—an early version of luxury boxes—while behind home plate the Ladies Pavilion, a forerunner of tiered grandstands, reserved space for the fair sex and their escorts. Where I sit today, in left field, was known then as the "bleaching boards," a nod to the sun's effect on the benches.

As the grounds crew gives the Pac Bell infield its pregame hosing, I check a sports page for pitching matchups and late-breaking player news. Like the Giants, the first pros were generally glorified by the press. But they also took some heat from local scribes. "The Red Stockings are professionals," one paper sniffed, "who do nothing else, and are paid for doing that." Paid too much, more than a few people thought, for playing a boy's game as their so-called profession. But the visitors' flashy play silenced most naysayers, and their unflappable demeanor was impressive. They were lauded for never showing "a single instance of exulting over their opponents, carping at the play of each other, nor disapproval at the decision of the umpire—everything being received as a matter of course."

Umps today should have it so good.

The game at Pac Bell gets under way, and as the innings pass before me, time blurs and seems to curl in on itself, the disparate eras blending on the diamond sward. Even the players seem to ebb and flow: the Red Stockings' clear equivalent to Barry Bonds was George Wright, a future Hall of Famer who was celebrated as the game's first superstar; at first base stood J. T. Snow's counterpart, Charley "Human Bushel Basket" Gould, who handled "finger-breaker" throws—in those days without benefit of a glove; second sacker Charles Sweasy shared Jeff Kent's penchant for clutch home runs with men on base; speedy Andy Leonard, a foreign-born outfielder (County Cavan, Ireland), matched Marvin Benard (Bluefields, Nicaragua) in both his diminutive size and his intense play.

I stand with the crowd for "Take Me Out to the Ballgame." The song hadn't been written yet in 1869, but at the Recreation Grounds there was already a seventh-inning intermission for "refreshments"—mostly of the liquid variety. The wind gusts briefly now and as a hot dog wrapper blows before me, I'm reminded that the old-time visitors complained about chill afternoon winds that numbed their hands and blew sand in their eyes and carried fly balls beyond their straining reach.

But fans back then weren't about to let anything dampen their spirit as they turned out in unprecedented numbers to watch the nation's top players perform in their new park. "The season has commenced," one newspaper noted, "with an energy unknown before."

One hundred and thirty-one years later, sharing the sunlit afternoon with a sellout crowd in the Giants' splendid new ballpark—as the ferries dock and the light-rail cars unload their fares and the new digital elite stroll down from South Park—it seems to me that the sentiment fits perfectly once again.

Berkeley writer Darryl Brock is the author of two baseball-related historical novels: the national best-seller *If I Never Get Back* and the recently released *Havana Heat*.

The barge out on the Bay begins shooting rockets that trail colored smoke. As the smoke trails drift down into the park, hundreds of balloons rise from the field to meet them. "It's a miracle," says the city's former poet laureate, Beat legend Lawrence Ferlinghetti. "It's all a miracle."

Once the barge leaves McCovey Cove it's as if someone has fired the starter's gun at a regatta. Speedboats and yachts, dinghies and sailboats, all stream back in toward the park. Even waterbound fans, it seems, want the best seats.

Giants president Peter Magowan steps to the mike and welcomes fans by reminding them that the ownership group had ten goals when it purchased the beloved but troubled team in late 1992. With the opening of the park, he says, only one goal remains: a World Series victory, and Magowan promises the fans he won't rest until that dream, too, is made real. Then he and Executive Vice President Larry Baer each throw out a ceremonial ball, and it's game time.

Left-hander Kirk Rueter hurls the official first pitch—a ball, outside, to the Dodgers' Devon White—and retires the side handily. In the bottom of the second, catcher Doug Mirabelli gives fans a

THE KEY WORD IS *PARK* by *Leonard Koppett*

A PARK IS A PLACE SET ASIDE for relaxation, recreation, and leisure; a respite from the city's busyness; an oasis of attractive landscaping outfitted with recreational equipment. For a century and a half, Americans have always thought and spoken of "going to the ballpark," whatever the formal name of the facility happened to be. New York, in due course, had its Yankee Stadium and Ebbets Field. And the Giants always played in the Polo Grounds. Major-league baseball facilities in many places were called "Field" or "Grounds."

Field is so ambiguous, though. There are football, soccer, and lacrosse fields, and the modifier *baseball* is required to make it specific. And *stadium* is a self-aggrandizing term that consciously conjures up the structures of antiquity (like Rome's famous Colosseum), which were used as much for mayhem and ceremony as for mere games.

But *park* means something else. A good ballpark starts with a carefully manicured playing surface, large enough for effective pitching, not too large for enough home runs and with outfield fences that provide a variety of shapes and angles.

As a baseball writer for more than fifty years, I've operated in twenty-eight ball-parks no longer in use, and eleven that still are. Since 1992, there have been a dozen new ones. I've gone to work in stadiums (Yankee, Cleveland, Dodger, Milwaukee, Atlanta, and Washington's Griffith, among others), fields (Chicago's Wrigley, Cincinnati's Crosley, Pittsburgh's Forbes, Boston's Braves), and eventually domes. I loved the intimacy of Ebbets Field, the peculiarities of the Polo Grounds, and the nobility of Yankee Stadium (more noble in the past than in its present form). In my mind, though, they were always just ball-parks, which is what made them special.

Baseball's first wave of ballparks came before World War I. They were appropriately intimate with respect to the playing field, had interesting contours, and were pretty near downtown. But the seats were narrow, the aisles even narrower, the views

blocked by structural beams, the concession stands usually inadequate, and the locker rooms and dugouts pretty rudimentary. Media facilities were jury-rigged afterthoughts that gradually improved. Luxury boxes did not exist. Lights for night games were tacked on in the 1930s and 1940s and were not always first-rate.

The cookie-cutter multipurpose ovals, designed and built in the 1960s, were no solution. They had no posts, but the seats were too far from the action. The stadiums themselves were too far from the action, some of them being put in outlying areas for the sake of parking space. Their symmetrical and stereotyped shape was simply wrong for baseball. They were a mistake all around and are now being abandoned.

Relocation and expansion made it worse. Teams moved into domes and stadiums and coliseums. By the end of the 1980s only two real "parks" remained in the majors: Fenway and Comiskey. (Once it was double-decked all the way around—for football's sake—Candlestick became a stadium, no matter what it was called.)

In the 1990s, though, we finally got it right: the old model in shape, atmosphere,

intimacy, and interesting contours, combined with thoroughly modern engineering—no posts, good aisles, the best lighting systems, high-tech scoreboards, and all the rest. Baltimore came first, then Cleveland, then Dallas (Arlington), then Denver. But San Francisco's Pac Bell is the perfect realization of the concept, incorporating all the best of its predecessors, with incomparable vistas.

It combines the best traditional features of a tradition-steeped experience with the most modern amenities, which suits a television-age audience accustomed to being entertained amid the comforts of their homes. More important, it comes closer to the heart of what "going to the ballpark" means than any other experiment of the past forty years.

Leonard Koppett has covered sports, as a reporter and columnist, for the *New York Herald Tribune*, the *New York Post*, the *New York Times*, the *Sporting News* and Bay Area newspapers. He has written more than a dozen sports books and is the only sportswriter in the writers' wing of both the Baseball and Basketball Halls of Fame.

taste of Pac Bell Ball, hitting a blast roughly 420 feet to the far corner of right center—for a triple. Mirabelli's bomb would have been a homer in almost any other park in the country, but the none-too-speedy catcher's unlikely three-bagger foretells the future: it will be triples and doubles, not home runs into the Bay over the short right-field wall, that will distinguish the new park's brand of baseball.

There are home runs, too, this first day. But sadly for the Giants, three of them come from Dodger journeyman Kevin Elster, and the team drops its home opener 6-5.

Still, fans go away happy with their first look at their new ballpark. Perhaps the highest praise comes from an elderly fan, who in his day had seen all the hallowed old parks in the country, from Pittsburgh's Forbes Field to Cincinnati's Crosley to the Polo Grounds and Ebbets Field in New York. The Giants have done the impossible in building Pac Bell, he tells broadcaster Mike Krukow: "This park has an old soul."

"It will be quite a while before we loosen our grip on Pac Bell and see it as just another place with bases and fences and a scoreboard. Things beautiful are rarely so easily dismissed." —Bob Padecky, *Santa Rosa Press Democrat*

Two weeks later, some fans think about selling their souls to get the team its first home win. By the time the Giants get their first victory at Pac Bell, the Atlanta Braves have thirteen home wins, the St. Louis Cardinals, eleven. Tongue only partway in cheek, a San Francisco newspaper consults a priest, a psychic, a parapsychologist, an astrologer, a tarot card reader, and an exorcist to diagnose the team's troubles. The experts from the spirit world agree: the Giants' fortunes will improve eventually.

And, of course, they do.

On April 29 the Giants beat the Montreal Expos 2-1, for their first Pac Bell Park win, a pitching duel that features a game-winning home run by Barry Bonds. The team goes 5- 2 on the home stand, a very telling harbinger of the season to come.

Overleaf: Images
of Opening Day,
April II, 2000.

4 Behind the Clubhouse Walls

CLUBHOUSE MANAGER MIKE MURPHY, A FORTY-TWO-YEAR GIANTS VETERAN, feels like he has died and gone to heaven. The locker room at Candlestick had the feel of an old-time gym: crowded, drafty, a little dank. At Pac Bell, the locker room has all the warmth and comfort of somebody's den, furnished in dark cherrywood and neutral gray carpeting, with televisions, couches, and easy chairs. And with fifty-two lockers in the digs, it's a snap to make room for newcomers called up from the minors. In past years, Murphy had to borrow lockers from the San Francisco 49ers to accommodate late-season arrivals, squeezing them into the team's already cramped quarters. Now the call-ups have the same spacious, wood closets for their uniforms, street clothes, family photos, and CDs as the players who have been here all season—a touch that can't help but pay off on the field.

The move from Candlestick to Pac Bell proved to be a psychological boost for everyone, says Murphy, a batboy at Seals Stadium who worked his way up to clubhouse manager in 1979 and has been honored by having the new clubhouse named after him. "It was like moving from an old house to a penthouse," he says with a smile.

Step into that "penthouse" before any given game and you find Barry Bonds reclining in his black leather massage chair, watching his twenty-seven-inch TV. Kirk Rueter sits on the couch reading a newspaper, while Robb Nen heads to the kitchen for a snack.

For six months, this is essentially home for the players, and Murphy makes sure it feels that way. He stocks the kitchen with industrial-strength boxes of Frosted Flakes and keeps the steam

Gone are the steel lockers and concrete floors; Mike Murphy, now in his fifth decade with the team, runs a clubhouse of wall-to-wall carpeting and rich wood closets. Opposite: Dusty Baker's office gives him room to have visitors while he makes out his lineup card, like the one from the August 19 shellacking of the Braves, which featured two bombs from Ellis Burks.

tables piled with steak and chicken at lunch and dinnertime. Guys who show up for breakfast even find the waffle irons warmed and ready. And plenty do show up, Murphy says. In the past, players reported to Candlestick when required to—for stretching exercises, batting practice, or team meetings. Now they come early and stay late.

Murphy has a bigger office here than the tiny broom closet he used at Candlestick. It's big enough to display one of his most cherished possessions: an autographed painting of the baseball greats who have hit more than 500 home runs, with Hank Aaron in the center. Murphy is rarely

"It's good to be home." —Giants manager Dusty Baker

alone in the office. Most days before game time, either Willie McCovey or Willie Mays holds court here. Players walk in and out, some shy, some cocky, all of them anxious to soak up the Hall of Famers' presence, as though baseball success were contagious. Given that the Giants have more Hall of Famers than any other franchise in history (twenty-eight, including manager John McGraw), it just may well be.

Across the way is the office of manager Dusty Baker. He, too, has moved up from his cramped quarters at Candlestick, and before every game he meets with reporters in his office, answering questions about roster additions as he fills out a line-up card or holds his son, Darren, on his lap. Baker has room not just for a desk but for a couch and two matching upholstered chairs, a refrigerator, a bookshelf, and his son's tricycle. And in one corner the Giants built him his own locker, as befits an

The scoreboard operators gather updates through a laptop computer hookup, then post the results the low-tech way. Opposite: Wearing their fathers' numbers, batboys Daniel and Nicholas Gardner and Isaac Benard chase after the biggest kid at Pac Bell, Lou Seal.

intimidating All-Star-turned-manager who still wears his wristbands, even though it's been more than fifteen years since his last official at bat.

What distinguishes Baker's office, however—and so many other corners of the park—are not the luxurious amenities, but the old baseball photographs and paintings. Behind the desk hang three great photos of Jackie Robinson. On the wall above the couch, a photocollage of memorabilia belonging to Negro Leagues star James "Cool Papa" Bell—Bell's sunglasses, his glove, an old taped-up bat, and a baseball he autographed. You also notice that there are as many shots of Baker's family— son Darren, daughter Natosha, wife Melissa, his parents, and siblings—as of baseball stars.

This all fits: more than any other major-league outfit, the Giants cherish and welcome family. The team has become nationally known for the high number of players' and coaches' sons who serve as batboys. Barry Bonds, Ellis Burks, Mark Gardner, Marvin Benard, as well as coaches Robby Thompson, Dave Righetti, and Juan Lopez regularly have their kids in the dugout. There's even a

playroom for the kids just across from the clubhouse, with a microwave, a sofa, a picnic table, and art supplies. Most of the children have lockers there, too, just like their dads.

All these behind-the-scenes amenities, of course, are meant to keep players happy and to improve morale. But Pac Bell Park has several state-of-the-art features designed specifically to hone baseball skills.

Digital guru: Coach Carlos Alfonso checks a replay from the team's digital video-coaching system, which uses broadcast television feeds, supplemental cameras, and a vast database.

On a Saturday morning after a night game, the field is closed off as groundskeepers cope with the effects of a rare September rainstorm. But players still get their swings in, thanks to the team's spacious indoor batting cages. At Candlestick they shared one outdoor cage with the visiting team; here, adjacent to its clubhouse, each team has a cage in which up to four players can bat at a time.

Coaches Gene Clines and Robby Thompson monitor the swings and give advice as batters

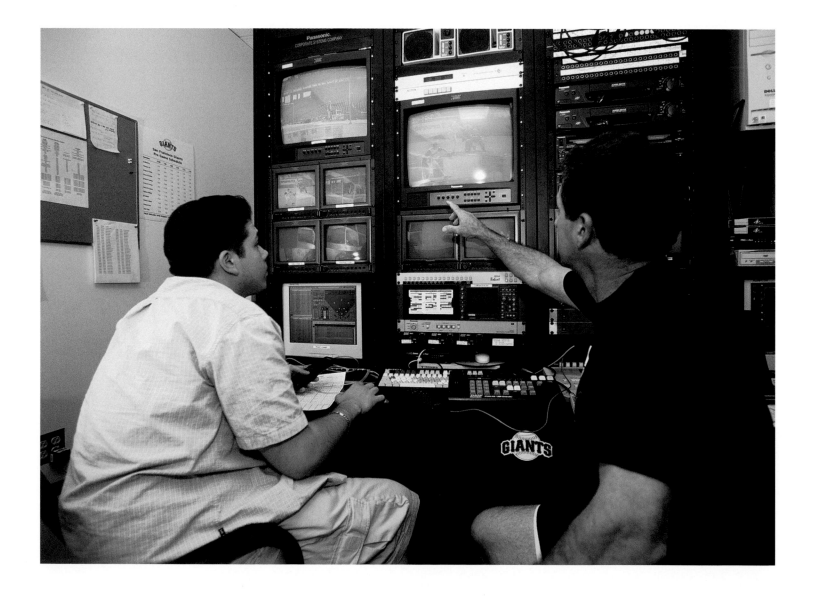

A MISSHAPEN GEM *by Ron Fimrite*

F. SCOTT FITZGERALD, no die-hard fan he, once described baseball as "a game bounded by walls which kept out novelty or danger, change or adventure." I can see what he's driving at: walls do get in the way, particularly of hits to the gap. And yet, he's missing an essential truth about ballparks, and that is that walls can add excitement to the game if they're in the right place—which is to say, not in the same place everywhere. And therein lies the beauty of Pac Bell Park, a masterwork of asymmetry, where fences to the left and right of center field are deeper than the one in dead center, where the left-field line stretches thirty feet longer than the right, and where the fence in left field is eight feet high, while the brick wall in right rises twenty-five feet. And where else will you find something called a Splash Hit?

We are blessed with a ballpark so idiosyncratic that it cannot be mistaken for another. Even in these relatively enlightened times, when all the new parks flaunt their individuality, ours stands proudly apart. We should be grateful for such places, for in the dark ages of ballpark architecture—the 1960s and 1970s—there was a numbing sameness to what baseball historian Michael Gershman called its "concrete doughnuts." These monoliths, many of which unfortunately survive, were almost geometrically identical. Consider that of the thirteen parks built between 1962 and 1973, nine had foul-line measurements in both left and right field of exactly 330 feet. The shortest of the thirteen measured 329 feet down the line, the longest, 338. The deepest power alley, either left or right, in any of these parks was 385 feet, the shallowest, 370. Eight of the alleys fell between 375 and 385 feet. The deepest center field of the Unlovely Thirteen was 420 feet, the shallowest, 400. Five measured exactly 400 feet. About as much imagination went into the planning of these homogenous structures as into the building of the ticky-tacky boxes of postwar suburbia.

Contrast them with the classic ballparks of baseball antiquity. At one time, there was a difference of more than 100 feet between the center fields of the cavernous Polo Grounds and cozy Ebbets Field. At the same time, it was only 279 feet down the left-field line at the Polo Grounds—and that meager distance was diminished another 20 feet because of the upper-deck overhang—while it was 405 at Griffith Stadium in Washington, DC. The Polo Grounds was built like a bathtub, Griffith Stadium like a hexagon.

Such disparities added dimension to the game. Certainly, there were cheap home runs, but there was also the excitement of watching balls roll forever into the vast power alleys of the Polo Grounds and Yankee Stadium. And think of the catches! Willie Mays executed his famous over-the-shoulder grab of Vic Wertz's 1954 World Series drive some 445 feet from home plate. In 1937, Joe DiMaggio caught a 451-footer hit by Hank Greenberg at Yankee Stadium. It was said that Joe was waiting patiently for the ball behind the monuments in center before it finally descended into his glove. That, of course, was the old Yankee Stadium, before the 1974-1975 "renovation" deprived it of character.

Balls hit that far won't stay within Pac Bell's walls. But we are going to see scores of doubles and triples snaked into those corridors in left and right center, some of them hit by such plodders as Giants catcher Doug Mirabelli. Before the 2000 season, Mirabelli had hit exactly zero major-league triples; he hit two at Pac Bell. Home runs are all well and good, particularly those that plop into the Bay, but the gapper provides the prolonged thrills.

How fortunate we are to have a ballpark alive with angles and corners, nooks and crannies, a building that is at one and the same time both beautiful and misshapen.

Ron Fimrite has been writing for *Sports Illustrated* for thirty years. He is currently writing a history of the San Francisco Olympic Club.

THE FIRST GLOVE *by Dave Newhouse*

THE WINDOW FELT WARM against my nose. It was August, my eleventh birthday was days away, and I was in love with the glove behind the glass. It was a Rawlings glove, a Roy Smalley model. I went inside Smith's-on-the-Circle, the Palo Alto sporting goods store, and tried on the glove for the umpteenth time. Then I ran to my father's store and, eliminating all element of birthday surprise, begged him to buy me the $10.95 glove. When I turned eleven, he took me to Smith's and purchased it.

My first glove.

How I loved its size, its smell, its feel. I didn't know much about Roy Smalley, but he must have had good taste to lend his name to so perfect a glove.

I kept that glove for six years, then, mindlessly, lost it. I've never forgiven myself. It felt worse than losing my first girlfriend.

If you're passionate about baseball, you remember your first glove like I do. So when I first glimpsed The Glove looming behind left field at Pac Bell, I thought instantly of my Roy Smalley model, even though they are dissimilar.

My glove had four fingers and a thumb. The Glove has three fingers and a thumb. I actually had a three-finger glove as a youth, an heirloom that Dad found somewhere. My only problem: I could never figure out where to put my fourth finger.

Retro stadiums are the new fashion in baseball, but no team has hit a home run architecturally quite like the Giants. For me, The Glove is the best thing about the best park in baseball. And I'm not alone in feeling a connection to it.

"My first glove was a three-finger," says Giants broadcaster Mike Krukow. "That was with me until my hand rotted through it seven years later. But The Glove lit me up."

"You see that Glove and you flash back to a game you played as a kid. It's almost spiritual," says fellow broadcaster Duane Kuiper. "I thought it was real leather."

Even from up close, this icon—which stands twenty-six feet high, thirty-two feet wide, and twelve feet deep and weighs twenty thousand pounds—looks like actual leather. Worn leather, with all the creases and scars of an antique.

But how do you build the King Kong of baseball gloves and make it look so real? That task fell to Ron Holthuysen of Scientific Arts Studio in Berkeley. He had one primary model: a 1940s four-finger number that belonged to the father of Giants general counsel Jack Bair. But while rummaging through a thrift store, Holthuysen found a 1927 three-finger glove.

"I looked at different models," he says, "but I thought this shape was more appealing than the four-finger glove with the big basket. It was a beautiful, old-age glove . . . the general feel of the sandlot. The Giants loved the idea."

To make the idea real, Holthuysen worked with concept designer Gerard Howland of the Floating Company. They studied Bair's glove through a microscope to duplicate the texture of the leather, and then used a laser scanner on the three-finger one to digitally model the shape of The Glove.

Finally, after consulting with structural engineer Dick Dreyer of Culley and Associates, they built The Glove out of steel, covered it with fiberglass and topped it with a claylike epoxy. Every wrinkle was sculpted, and marine rope provided the finishing touch for the stitching.

Now, The Glove sits high above the left-field bleachers, 501 feet from home plate. Is it conceivable that a home run, perhaps struck by Mark McGwire, could land in its pocket? "From about third base, maybe," says Giants left fielder Barry Bonds. "You'd need a .22 with a scope to hit it."

Just as well. It should be untouched. I accidentally left my first glove at a park after a teenage softball game. It never turned up. Smith's-on-the-Circle closed years ago. Roy Smalley was followed into the big leagues by Roy Smalley Jr.

Time moves on. But The Glove will stand for decades—brand new in its oldness—to refresh our minds of when baseball first held us captive.

Dave Newhouse, a sportswriter for forty years, is a columnist for the Oakland Tribune/ Alameda Newspaper Group and the author of five books.

David Lowenstein, the Umpire's Room assistant, checks a shipment of official National League baseballs. Overleaf: Each team gets a vast indoor batting cage at Pac Bell—just don't tell the visitors it's below sea level.

swat baseballs into large green nets. Outside the cage, third baseman Bill Mueller awaits his turn, practicing his swing alone in a hallway. For fans, one of the park's best features is a wide window that lets them watch the action in the batting cages. But sometimes Clines draws the drapes, a sign to onlookers that a struggling player needs his privacy to work the kinks out of his swing.

While Clines and Thompson coach players the old-fashioned way, Carlos Alfonso uses the best technology the twenty-first century has to offer: the team's digital video-coaching system, which is unrivaled in professional sports. Alfonso heads a squad of coaches and technicians responsible for recording every pitch of every Giants game on videotape, organizing it digitally, and putting it on DVDs and CD-ROMs so that players have easy access to it.

Teams have used video coaching for years: they tape games and then let hitters and pitchers review their play for trouble spots. But the system is cumbersome. It forces players to fast-forward through hours of game tape to view one at bat, and it requires coaches to keep track of literally thousands of videotapes in already-crowded clubhouses.

Pac Bell Park—just a long fly ball from Silicon Valley—took a great leap forward with its elaborate digital system. Every game, whether at home or on the road, is captured via satellite or local television stations and recorded on videotape. Inside Pac Bell, coaching cameras in four locations—center field, high above home plate, and behind first and third base—supplement the television record of home games.

Technicians enter every pitch and its location into the computer system while the games are recorded. In a late-August game against the Pittsburgh Pirates, for instance, the cameras catch Ellis

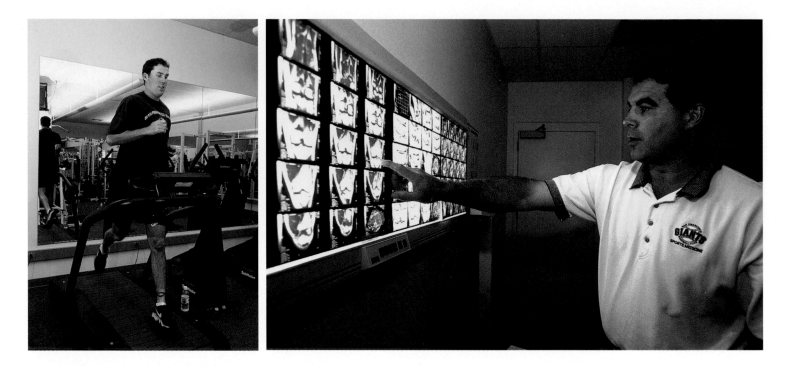

Pitcher Joe Nathan tunes up on the treadmill, while head trainer Stan Conte checks X-rays down the hall. Opposite: Conte's training regimen and state-of-the-art facilities like the hydrotherapy system helped make the Giants the healthiest team in the major leagues—just ask No. 23's knees.

Burks hitting an outside fastball on a 3-1 count for an RBI single off Pirates pitcher Jimmy Anderson. The system then organizes the game digitally so that the next time the Giants face the Pirates, Burks can call up that very at bat and watch it on a computer monitor.

In fact, Burks can watch himself up against any pitcher he's faced all year. In the computer server room sits the TeraCart—a digital "jukebox" that can store four terabytes of information, at least three years' worth of Giants games—which contains the team's entire season on 750 DVDs. The system sorts video files by pitcher, letting a player watch every at bat against, say, the Braves' Tom Glavine; by date, showing all the at bats on August 20, when the Giants suffered a rare home game loss; or by outcome, letting a player watch only those at bats in which he hit a home run, or struck out, or faced a full count. With a few mouse clicks, the player can move on to Greg Maddux and study his fastball, his change-up, or his pickoff move to first.

The system helps pitchers, too. While one technician records the just-completed game, another customizes individual CDs for pitchers in an upcoming series against the Chicago Cubs. Each pitcher can watch every Cubs at bat against him from the whole year. He might watch in conference with pitching coach Dave Righetti, a big fan of the digital system, or take it home and view it on a handheld device customized for the Giants by Panasonic.

Coach Alfonso believes the digital system helped players learn the idiosyncrasies of the new park more quickly. Players watch fly balls get knocked down by the wind again and again; they see how a ball that everybody thinks is leaving the park actually lands twenty yards in front of the warning track: "It reinforces what you learn every day," Alfonso says.

The best news for the 2000 Giants wasn't their gorgeous accommodations or their digital coaching system. It was the fact that the vast majority of players stayed healthy all year. Collectively, the Giants spent fewer days on the disabled list than any other team in baseball. The future health

"Sometimes late at night we take out the surgical pictures of his knees and say, 'There's no way a person with these knees can do what he did tonight.'" —Giants head trainer Stan Conte, on Ellis Burks

of stars like Barry Bonds and Robb Nen will owe a lot to the new park, where state-of-the-art weight and workout rooms, a hydrotherapy system, and a training center let Stan Conte and his staff minister to the healthy and the struggling alike.

Behind the action: Aaron Fultz relaxes in the clubhouse; a wall of team notices; the press corps gets a prime view of the field; and the broadcast crew gets multiple views. Opposite: Woody and wood—a locker that can belong only to Kirk Rueter and bats for several Giants.

Conte credits the team for sparing no expense on training facilities for the new ballpark. His wide-windowed training room is strategically located at the center of the action, down the hall from the locker room, where his staff can watch players on the treadmill, in the weight room, in the hydrotherapy room, on massage tables, or even while they're being examined by team physicians.

At Candlestick the weight room was a small area that the 49ers used for press conferences, so the equipment had to be moved out whenever the Niners were home during the football season. At Pac Bell the spacious workout area combines free weights and machines, with low-impact treadmills, StairMasters, and crosstrainers in the corner.

Next door is the hydrotherapy room, the centerpiece of which is the Swim-Ex, an indoor pool that lets players swim or run against a challenging current. Because of its size, it had to be built into the clubhouse first, and then the gray-tiled floor and walls were built around it. Players with knee problems jog in the Swim-Ex for a tough workout, and those recovering from injuries can swim or run in it to maintain their conditioning before they're ready to work out on treadmills or the field. "We know that players want to play," Conte says. "We help them distinguish between pain and injury, and we give them the facts they need to make educated choices."

"Throughout the game, there's almost a line dance as people take their lap around the park. And it's not always going in the same direction. But they don't miss a pitch when they're taking that lap."

—Duane Kuiper, Giants broadcaster and former Giants second baseman

The training room can be a tough place for a player: it's where he must bare his soul and ask for help, and if he doesn't trust the training staff, he may avoid it—and wind up getting really hurt. But a well-run training room can become a sanctuary where a player is able to get away from the media, relax, and learn how to stay healthy.

That's the kind of training room Conte proudly maintains, and the proof is how players congregate here, sometimes hanging out and talking long after their postgame workouts and treatments are over. Safe in their private corner of Pac Bell heaven.

5 *This Is How We Play the Game*

BEFORE THE 2000 SEASON, THE *SPORTING NEWS* GROUPED PAC BELL PARK WITH Houston's new Enron Field as a disaster area for pitchers and warned of an epidemic of wiry infielders chasing the Astros' Jeff Bagwell and the Giants' Barry Bonds for their teams' home-run records. The park's 309-foot fence in right field had many baseball commentators calling Pac Bell ground zero for cheap home runs, a hitter's paradise to rival Coors Field.

Giants pitching coach Dave Righetti didn't want his staff believing the hype, so he told his pitchers a professionally justified, ethically defensible, creative variation on the truth—what some might call, for lack of a better term, a lie. It was exactly what they needed to hear. "I told them this was a pitcher's park," Righetti recalls. "Even though everybody said it was a hitter's park, I really didn't know for sure." As it turned out, the former Giants reliever was just about dead right when he reassured his guys about their chances at Pac Bell. For many people the biggest surprise of the inaugural season was that Pac Bell turned out to be, if not a pitcher's park, certainly an extremely fair park—and one where Giants pitchers prospered.

Of course, the whole team thrived in the 2000 season, compiling the best overall record in the major leagues and sharing the title for the best home record in baseball. But in hindsight, the success enjoyed by Giants pitchers at Pac Bell makes some sense.

For one thing, the park is on the waterfront, where the air is moist, and during most of the season balls didn't carry that well, especially at night. The wind normally blows in from right field and out to left center, keeping balls hit toward the short fence hanging in the air. In the end, the

Baseball pundits forgot to check with people like Livan Hernandez before calling Pac Bell Park a hitter's paradise. In the inaugural season, Giants pitchers led the majors in shutouts— Hernandez pitched two, back to back.

Giants and their opponents hit far more home runs over the left-field fence than to that seductively close right-field porch.

On the plus side for the hitters, the scanty foul territory means that balls that might have been caught for outs at Candlestick now drift into the stands. And while the wind is less fierce than at the 'Stick, it still wreaks havoc with pop-ups. More than a few seemingly easy fly balls fell for hits at Pac Bell—and most of them fell for the Giants, as visitors seemed slow to catch on to the wind patterns.

Giants players learned quickly not to be fooled by the calm that prevails around home plate. If you want to know what the wind is like on the field, check out the umpire behind second base: if his gray pant legs are flapping in the breeze, it's going to be a wild day for defense at Pac Bell Park.

The real question about the park was whether the Giants would get to play there at all. Even after the team secured the site and the city signed off on the plans, the Giants still had to negotiate

THE LOVE OF THE GAME *by Chris Berman*

IF SAN FRANCISCO WAS the place for a cultural love-in during the 1960s, then Pac Bell Park is the place for a baseball love-in during the 2000s. Like warm and cozy Haight-Ashbury back then, it's all about the complete experience—which begins on the Plaza before you even enter the ballpark: Giants fans talking to fellow Giants fans, many of whom they had never met before. Everyone getting excited about the whole day or evening about to unfurl inside.

Don't get me wrong. I loved Candlestick Park, and will always love it. But hanging around outside is something that rarely happened there—not like this.

I'm still not sure how they made Pac Bell Park so small, and yet so big. Small enough that you can walk around the entire park without missing the entire game. Big enough to put almost 41,000 fans in the seats.

How about those Arcade seats on top of the right-field wall? There is no better spot in fair territory anywhere in any park. And what about directly below those seats, where the modern-day knothole gang can watch the Giants play for free? Boy, would John McGraw have loved that.

Speaking of McGraw, the history of the old New York Giants is displayed proudly along with the history of the San Francisco Giants, like never before. A youngster might ask about Willie Mays, Willie McCovey, Juan Marichal, and Orlando Cepeda. And his or her dad might be able to answer the question—and tell a few stories. But when a youngster sees all the old photos and murals of McGraw, Christy Mathewson, Bill Terry, and Mel Ott, and asks Dad about *them,* he won't be so ready with the answer. Now, two generations can peer through time together and discover that for a century the Giants' history has been as rich as they come.

Of course, we come to Pac Bell to see the Giants play. On Opening Day I was lucky enough to sit behind the plate, where I know I was closer to the catcher than the pitcher was—and I'm well aware that the pitcher was sixty feet, six inches away. Not all the seats are that close. But I'm willing to bet that most every seat at Pac Bell is closer to the play than a comparable seat in any other ballpark. Want to almost touch the relievers warming up in the bullpens? No problem here.

I've long felt that San Francisco Giants fans were the most unheralded, loyal fans in baseball. Now there's a place for them to go en masse every day to prove it.

If San Francisco is the best city in America for a love-in—or just to live-in—shouldn't it have a comparable place to watch baseball? In Pac Bell Park, the answer is a resounding yes.

Since 1979, Chris Berman has been the mainstay of ESPN. He is the anchor of the network's *SportsCenter* and a play-by-play commentator on its Major League Baseball broadcasts. He has five times been selected National Sportscaster of the Year—and is proud to have a patch of Candlestick outfield grass growing in his backyard.

On Opening Day, Dusty Baker and Dodgers manager Davey Johnson exchange lineups and discuss the quirky ground rules of Pac Bell before the first game.

the details with Major League Baseball (MLB). To say that was not easy would be kind. The task of integrating league demands with local laws and the idiosyncrasies of the waterfront site proved as challenging as mastering the knuckleball.

First of all, MLB wanted the Giants to build a perfectly symmetrical ballpark, with an unchanging eight-foot-high outfield wall. Peter Magowan and Larry Baer wanted very asymmetric dimensions, with an outfield wall that was high in some spots and low in others, much like Boston's Fenway Park. Eventually the Giants prevailed.

The next big problem: That right-field porch, again. Early designs of the park put home plate near the Lefty O'Doul Bridge, about where the right-field foul pole now stands. But the team brought in Bruce White, a professor of aeronautical science from UC Davis, who said the field would have to be rotated to afford it protection from the wind. It quickly became clear, given the presence of the Bay, that the park was going to have a unique right-field corner.

Major-league officials wanted the fence to go right to the edge of the Bay, but coastal laws required public access to the waterfront. That meant the right-field wall would be a mere 309 feet from home plate, an open invitation to every Todd, Chris, and Alex with a bat. To compensate, the Giants agreed to make the wall twenty-five feet high—not quite Fenway's Green Monster, but tall enough to protect against so-called cheap home runs.

And there were other sticking points. The Giants wanted an intimate park, one with small foul areas, bullpens on the field (like Chicago's Wrigley), and fans on top of the action. But league officials worried about fan interference and the safety of fans and players alike. The team managed to avoid placing nets along the bleachers that at Wrigley keep fans from interfering with long fly balls, but they acceded to an MLB request that the seats be moved back a few feet in the right-field foul territory to give players more running room.

Some of the negotiated ground rules—like Pac Bell Park itself—have to be classified as "only in San Francisco." Far back in the right-center-field corner there's a brick wall that's above the bleacher seats but below the Arcade. If a ball hits that wall and bounces into the seats, it's a home run; but if it bounces back onto the field without hitting anything else (fans included), it's still in play. In right field, however, if a ball hits the green metal roof below the Arcade seats, you can tell it good-bye—it's a home run whether it bounces into the seats or falls back onto the field, touched by a fan or not.

The league also had its doubts about one of the park's most endearing aspects: the walkways from the dugouts to the clubhouses, which pass through a hallway where fans can stand. Ushers protect players before and after games, but a struggling pitcher yanked from the game or a batter

Giants lefties Bonds, Mueller, Snow, and Rios don't aim for the short porch; they spray hits all over the park. The squad's combined bats scored more runs than any Giants team in seventy years. Overleaf: On April 15, Barry Bonds leaps, and fifteen-year-old Rickie Navarette makes the catch. The design of Pac Bell Park makes fan interference a very real possibility.

pulled for a pinch hitter has to run a gauntlet of fans to get to the showers, and some MLB officials weren't sure that would work.

But the players got used to it, and now it's one of manager Dusty Baker's favorite features: "We see the fans more, and we also see the other people who work here—the vendors, the ushers, the security dudes. You can really see the life and the spirit of the park in all of them: the people who work here, and the fans. It lifts us up, the way our wins and losses are reflected in everybody. Of course, sometimes you've got to dodge a forklift on your way to work, but that's OK."

Rules aside, Giants players weren't sure they liked their new home when they first saw it. The outfield looked huge, center fielder Marvin Benard remembers: "But when you get out there, it's comfortable," he says. "It plays less dangerously than it looks."

It *does* look dangerous. Many major-league ball fields are just glorified triangles—two foul lines and a never-varying arc of an outfield wall creating a curved third side. Not so, Pac Bell Park. The Giants have themselves a heptagon—a seven-sided fielder's nightmare. And it's not just the short 309 feet to the right-field foul pole; it's the dogleg in right, at 365 feet; it's the wicked right-center corner, 421 feet away; and it's the 404-foot corner in the left-center power alley. Plus, there's a zany combination of surfaces out there—red brick walls, padded fences, chain-link fences, and that picturesque but tricky green metal roof below the Arcade. Balls take different bounces depending on where and what they hit, and the outfielders have to adjust to play the bounce off padding, brick, fence, or roof. Every home stand sees a surprise or two—but usually the surprises hurt the visitors

more than the home team. Giants outfielders, for instance, tend not to chase balls over their heads; wisely, they play them on a bounce off the fence to keep the damage to a double or, if the ball bounces back sharply, a long single. Opponents usually go after those fly balls, and all too often watch the Giants turn them into triples.

Hitters also find that the short right field isn't the boon they expected. Righties almost never hit it out, and lefties rarely do. It's no accident that lefty superstar Barry Bonds owns all six official Splash Hits (those hit by the Giants), and that Sammy Sosa is one of only four righties to slam a right-field home run in the entire first season.

Giants pitchers help make sure many balls don't make a water landing by pitching to the outside of the plate, to capitalize on the wide-open spaces and eccentric corners in the outfield. That the

SAFE AT HOME *by Ann Killion*

PACIFIC BELL PARK RESTS on a sub-structure of something more significant than black San Francisco Bay mud. The true foundation is a thousand failed plans, truckloads full of cynicism, and the potential of a million broken hearts.

My father's heart was secured forty-two years and ten blocks away from Third and King, the spot where Pac Bell now stands. In April of 1958, he stood on Montgomery Street in a ticker-tape swirl, his four-year-old son perched on his shoulders.

San Francisco was becoming a major-league town. A transplant from Minnesota, my father firmly believed that San Francisco was the best city in the United States. And on that day, he was there to help welcome the Giants and the best ballplayer—Willie Mays—to the best city.

At age fifty, my father found his team and he never let go. He formed a bond that seemed to imprint on his DNA. He passed down his team allegiance to his children, the same way he passed down his blue eyes and Irishman's wit.

He watched Mays, McCovey, and Marichal. He watched Jack Clark, LeMaster, and Minton. He went to Seals Stadium and to Candlestick Park. He was there at the 1961 All-Star Game when Stu Miller blew off the mound, at the 1962 World Series, and in 1989 when Candlestick shook to its core.

One afternoon in 1964, my father convinced my mother to go to Candlestick with him. It was a clear, blazing hot day in Marin County. So off they went, without sweaters, in summer outfits. By the sixth inning, in the old horseshoe ballpark, they were freezing. That was the notorious "fog-delay" game against the Dodgers. They fled, and it was many years and a few grandchildren before my mother could be convinced to go back.

Dad didn't attend a lot of games at Candlestick. For the most part, he was content to follow the Giants on the brown transistor radio that rarely left his breast pocket. As I climbed in his lap, I could hear Russ Hodges and Lon Simmons calling out balls and strikes from behind the Oxford cloth. As I got older, I ventured bravely off to Candlestick, bundled in a down jacket and weighed down with blankets my father thrust upon me.

Even if he wasn't at the ballpark, my father knew that his fate was intertwined with that cement bowl down at Candlestick Point. His team needed a better home.

As my father grew older, his team toyed with his affection. There was talk more than once about selling the Giants. In 1992, I took him to Candlestick, making a pilgrimage to what was supposed to be one of the last home games before the team moved to Florida. My father didn't say much, but it was clear what losing the team would mean to him.

So it was with joy—forty-two years almost to the day after he had stood on the corner of Montgomery and Post—that we made another pilgrimage, to bid another welcome. This time to the new home that would keep his team in the best city in the country. This time to a ballpark that his team deserved.

He made the trip in a wheelchair that day, and there was no four-year-old son perched on his shoulders. Instead, we brought along his grandson—my eight-year-old, who has inherited his grandfather's slight stature, his blue eyes, and his fondness for a black cap with orange stitching.

Together, three generations—the lifeblood of baseball—toured the ballpark. My father marveled at its beauty. We paid homage to the statue of Willie Mays, the man whose name began and ended all conversations in our house about athletic excellence.

My father looked at my son with an expression of slight envy. After all, my boy will be the first generation of baseball fans to think of Pac Bell as home.

Dad hasn't been to a game at the new park, but thanks to our tour, he can picture it in his head. He delights in hearing his grandchildren tell of sliding down the Coke bottle, of watching balls soar into the Bay.

And my father can watch his games peacefully, knowing that the team he welcomed to San Francisco almost half a century ago is finally secure. At home, at last.

Ann Killion is a Bay Area native and a sports columnist for the *San Jose Mercury News*. As a kid, she always had a black cap with orange stitching hanging in her closet.

backstop is so close behind the plate makes it tougher for a base runner to advance if one of those outside pitches becomes a wild pitch. And that close backstop gives pitchers another advantage by making the plate look bigger from the mound, says Righetti. "The park has places a pitcher can pitch to, and that's what makes it fair."

"It's a good place to pitch if you know how to do it." —Giants pitcher Livan Hernandez

It may play fair, but clearly the Giants have a resounding home-field advantage. And several theories have been offered to explain that. "Everyone comes in here and starts swinging for that right-field porch," says Benard, with a grin. "We know better now—it's easier said than done—and we've forgotten about it."

Chicago Cubs manager Don Baylor compares it to Boston's Green Monster: "You look out at the wall, and you swing for it, but you can't make it unless you have just the right swing."

Baylor shakes his head at how the Giants have taken to their park. "These guys had a huge advantage at Candlestick, where everybody else complained, and now they have one here, because they've learned how to play this place." Baylor predicts it'll take the rest of baseball years to catch on: "We play only six games a year here, but [the Giants] have eighty-one."

Most people also credit the park's sellout crowds. The Giants have 40,930 reasons, every game, to go all out at home: "It's the 'tenth man' factor, but it's something else," says Shawn Estes. "Guys show up here much more motivated to play. And the fans appreciate it. It's a rush to hear them cheering you when you've got the bases loaded and two outs and it's a 3-2 count. It's a rush to play here, period."

Nobody talks much about it, but there is probably a more subtle psychological advantage to the splendor of Pac Bell Park. Somehow, having the best park in baseball helped the Giants play like the best teams in baseball. For years their self-image was tied inextricably to Candlestick—they were a gritty blue-collar team, often pegged as underdogs and overachievers, tough-playing warriors who made the best of one of the worst parks in the major leagues. Early in the Dusty Baker era, particularly, the team was dismissed as a collection of journeymen rather than All-Stars, guys who played over their heads season after season thanks to the genius of their manager. The oft-repeated cliché bothered Baker as much as it did his players, but repetition helped give the backhanded compliment the ring of truth.

The only smoking allowed inside Pac Bell came from Robb Nen: in 66 innings, he struck out a staggering 92 batters; the rest of the men he faced managed to touch him for a measly .162 average.

But in their first season in a park fit for champions, the Giants played like champions. The national media came to marvel at their new home and wound up marveling at their victories. In the end, San Francisco and the entire country learned something crucial about Pacific Bell Park: this is a park built for October baseball.

6 *The Best Seats in the House*

SIT ON A BENCH IN THE GIANTS' DUGOUT AND YOU LOOK DIRECTLY ACROSS the field at one of Pac Bell Park's signature features: the Portwalk, just below the Arcade in right field, where passersby can peer through the fences and watch the game for free.

During weekend games against a hot team, the crowd at the Portwalk gates can get six-fans deep. Ushers are under orders to rotate people in and out every three innings, to make sure that everybody who wants to watch gets a chance, but it's almost never necessary. Most days a democratic baseball camaraderie prevails. Adults make way to let kids move up front, the tall tend to stand at the back, and the in-between often get creative: There was the medium-height man who put on his Rollerblades to see the action better, rather than elbow his way past a family in front of him: "I come here all the time on my lunch hour," he explained. "Let them have a chance."

Portwalk fans range from old Candlestick die-hards to skateboarders taking a break, young pierced-and-tattooed Giants fans who dig getting to catch a game for free, and middle-aged Sunday strollers who just happen by. They watch the action on the field or peek behind the scenes into the manual scoreboard above them, where a crew of operators pace a catwalk to update out-of-town scores. The Giants pipe in KNBR so fans don't miss a play, and a Doggie Diner cart just outside sells hot dogs, peanuts, and Cracker Jack to make the experience complete.

The experience is totally baseball, but it's totally singular, too. In the first season Portwalk fans got to see visiting seals in McCovey Cove, misguided ducks and geese, and the occasional Bay swimmer. One day a horse and rider showed up at the gates. When an usher realized the rider wasn't a

Pac Bell combines the past and future. No other park features a "knothole" area where fans can watch for free or a way to beat the traffic and parking hassles by taking the ferry (overleaf) and docking at Marina Gate.

mounted cop, he asked the man what he was doing there. "I'm bringing my horse to its first ball game," he said, then moved along.

From a distance, the crowd behind each Portwalk fence appears to move in unison with the action, as if synchronized in a baseball dance. Fans line up at the best angle to watch the duel between pitcher and hitter. But when the bat hits the ball, the crowd drifts right, to the next fence in order to

"You knew you were at the 'Stick when the fog rolled in, the wind kicked up, and you saw the center fielder cutting open a caribou to survive the ninth inning." —Bob Sarlatte, comedian and field announcer for the San Francisco 49ers

watch the outfielder try to make the play. Then everybody shuffles to the left to see the throw to first base. Finally they settle back into their original position. The next batter steps to the plate and the dance begins again.

High above the Portwalk in right field, it's clear that some of the cheapest seats afford the best views. Climb to the very top corner of Section 302 in the View Level and you find a pair of seats by themselves: Row 17, Seats 1 and 2. From here you can see everything: the ferryboats unloading their passengers below, the full length of the Bay Bridge stretching into the distance, the city skyline peeking above the King Street roof, and best of all, the flight of a white ball moving against a changing background—from green field to dark blue sky to black water. The peak Pac Bell experience, another Barry Bonds Splash Hit.

"We had similar seats at the [Oakland] Coliseum years back, and it was a gyp," says Bob Trestler at his first Pac Bell game. "All we could see was Jose Canseco's back pocket. We looked at a seating chart and were disappointed when we realized how far up we'd be here, but we're sure not disappointed now."

This can be blanket country at night; the wind does kick up, but even on the worst nights it's no Candlestick. The fans up here are as raucous and passionate as any crowd that ever graced the 'Stick, and maybe more so than fans anywhere else at Pac Bell. There are more kids up here, too, since the seat prices make it easier to afford a family outing. And just a few sections over on this level is where J. T. Snow sponsors his "Snow Pack"—a block of seats reserved for underprivileged children and kids recovering from cancer.

Across the park, high above left field, the scene from Section 336 is different but no less stirring. Sutro Tower and Twin Peaks rise surreally above the Third Street roof of the ballpark, while a bright red barge slices the waters of McCovey Cove and rocks the sailboats in its wake. This may be the best place to watch a Splash Hit and follow its trajectory uninterrupted from the bat to the Bay.

Seats for thirty? Right this way. Where else can you watch a ball game from a cable car? This piece of San Francisco history served the Powell Street line for years. For a different panorama, the seats in the View Level live up to the name.

At most other ballparks, fans on the luxury level pay a premium for their boxes, and then have to watch games through open windows. Not at Pac Bell. Here, suiteholders have their choice of indoor or outdoor seating: each box comes with two rows of six seats outside, so those who want to can be right on top of the action. And most of them want to.

Aside from the exclusive seating, most people think the draw of the luxury level is the elegant food or the business center amenities for those who can't leave the office behind. But for true base-

"Pac Bell is as close to Wrigley Field as we're likely to get in the 21st century—except that the views on the North Side were never like this."

—David Lassen, sports columnist for the *Ventura County Star*

ball fans, nothing beats the beautiful lithographs of historic old baseball stadiums that are displayed in the hallways outside the Luxury Suites.

The paintings capture all the old urban parks, as well as the odd geographical details that made them special: the strange left-field corner in Washington's Griffith Stadium, which was built around a building the team wasn't able to buy and raze; the terraced outfield of Cincinnati's Crosley Field, which followed the line of the city's hills; and the bathtub shape of the Giants' former New York home, the Polo Grounds, with its amazing 483-foot stretch from home plate to the center-field fence. There's even Shibe Park in Philadelphia, whose "spite wall"—erected to keep fans in neighboring apartment houses from watching the game—inspired the Giants to build the Portwalk so there *would* be a place to watch for free.

As night falls in Pac Bell Park, there's no better place to watch the game than from behind home plate at the Club Level. When the setting sun shines just right on Oakland and Berkeley across the Bay, the windows of homes and offices sparkle against the green hills. The clouds above begin to darken, the Bay turns a deeper blue, and the currents in McCovey Cove seem to quicken. On the field below, the ball is whiter under the lights, the field even greener. As darkness descends, the cloud-scattered sky turns slate blue and pink.

On colder nights, you can sit at inside tables to feast on Edsel Ford Fong's Asian fusion or Joe Garcia's (named for an elevator operator at the park) chili and tacos. But it never gets that cold at the park, and what really pulls first-time Club Level visitors inside are the display cases full of team memorabilia going back to the New York days.

Giants president Peter Magowan is a native New Yorker who mourned when the team left for San Francisco, and it's no accident that under Magowan the team has re-embraced its storied

Sometimes you just have to rig up a "seat" outside the ballpark. Overleaf: Nothing escapes the sight of the folks at the top of Section 302. They can track balls heading for McCovey Cove, tankers steaming under the Bay Bridge, and planes descending to Oakland Airport.

The Coca-Cola Fan Lot attracts more attention than any other feature of the ballpark. You can scope out the giant Coke bottle; kids can take their swings inside the miniball-park; and it's the only place at Pac Bell where you can slide again and again and never get tagged out.

New York history and combined it with its San Francisco years to forge a new legacy. Reminders of the past have a prominence here that they never had at Candlestick: photos, team equipment, even reproductions of cartoons by legendary New York sports cartoonist Willard Mullin, whose work captured the sport for four decades.

"This is Ebbets Field with amenities. Griffith Stadium with a waterfront panorama. . . . Now it is fast becoming the pride of a city that likes to pretend it can be enraptured only by wacko causes or fringe literature."
—Larry Guest, *Orlando Sentinel*

Walk past the displays all the way to the left-field windows at the end of the Club Level, and you'll get one of the most unusual views of the park: the Coke bottle and the Glove that mark the Fan Lot, with palm trees and the Bay behind them and a never-ending parade of people.

The outfield has the greatest diversity of seats and diversions. Families love the Fan Lot: kids play Wiffle ball—they bat and run the bases at a miniature Pac Bell Park—while adults test their pitching arms at the speed booth. Panasonic installed a smaller Astrovision screen in the minipark, so young ballplayers can watch themselves on video just as they watch the Giants. Older kids who might hit too many balls out of the park can't bat, but they pitch to the little ones and help the ushers coach the youngsters on the game. You might even find team executive Larry Baer out here pitching to his kids and other future Giants stars.

Below the Fan Lot are the bleachers, where some of the team's most dedicated fans occupy some of the best seats in baseball at the lowest ticket price. Team officials were concerned about having the bleachers adjacent to the Fan Lot. "Bleacher bums" around the major leagues have the reputation of being baseball's rowdiest fans, and Jorge Costa, senior vice president of ballpark operations, worried that their proximity to the Fan Lot would produce a culture clash, a sort of *Sesame Street* meets *The Sopranos*. It didn't happen. Families love the bleachers because of the low ticket price, and the rowdy Candlestick die-hards who sit here seem to enjoy hanging with the newest generation of fans. Given that most Pac Bell homers are hit to left and left-center field, these may be the best seats in the house for souvenir seekers.

From cotton candy and a dog to sushi with a side of soybeans, the food at Pac Bell runs from traditional baseball fare to a range of gourmet cuisine.

Out toward right field, on the Arcade, are seats you'll find only in San Francisco. Here stands the Yahoo-sponsored cable car, and throughout the game ushers help kids climb on, ring the bell, and even watch the game from its wooden benches. The retired but lovingly restored car gives fans a perfect view of home plate, the pitcher, and batter. A sign in the cable car's window makes one rule very clear: no Dodgers fans allowed.

The people standing near the cable car aren't just stretching their legs or taking in the fabulous views. This is the Standing Room section, where fans pay just $8 to watch the game from the intimate right-field porch. Ushers work hard to keep their view unobstructed by asking other fans who are out for a stroll to walk behind them. (The ushers out here are also known for buying orders of garlic fries and sharing them with fans.)

In front of the standing room-section are the amazing Arcade seats, which hang out over the right-field corner and somehow feel even closer to the action than seats that are at field level. Follow the Arcade past the right-field foul pole and you make the turn into the Promenade, the Main Street of Pac Bell Park. From here, fans can watch the Giants bat even while standing in line for a beer or a Polish sausage—or an order of steamed *edamame* (soybeans, to you Braves fans).

"The first thing you're struck by at Pac Bell Park is that you're not being struck by an Arctic blast of wind." —Bud Geracie, *San Jose Mercury News*

Fans show up with baseball gloves throughout the park, but in the Field Club seats they're a necessity. Some of these seats are near enough to the action so that you can hear Jeff Kent tell J. T. Snow that the last pitch he saw was a slider. And you're definitely close enough to see the home plate umpire—it doesn't matter which one—drop his game face and grin when batboy Christopher Burks, barely four feet tall, sprints from the dugout to retrieve a stray ball and toss it into the stands.

Down the foul lines, the fans sit just a few feet away from the home and visitors' bullpens. They can see the sweat on Robb Nen's brow as he warms up on a hot afternoon, and on a windy night they may have to brush off the dust Nen kicks up when he plants his front foot just before his delivery. It's a distraction the fans are happy to cope with in exchange for being right on top of things.

Field Club fans get other perks: in the late innings, they can monitor the indoor batting cages and maybe glimpse Dusty Baker's strategy if he sends someone in to warm up for a pinch-hitting role. And from the same hallway they can watch their team file in from the dugout to the clubhouse, while the strains of "Who Let the Dogs Out?"—the team's late-season postvictory anthem—echo through the best little ballpark in baseball.

SORRY, THAT SEAT'S TAKEN *by Rick Clogher*

MY FATHER NEVER TOOK ME to the Polo Grounds. I'm not sure why. He grew up not far from it, having been born in Irish Harlem. And the Giants had always been his team.

He'd tell my brother and me about the great players he'd seen: Mel Ott and Johnny Mize, Johnny Antonelli and Sal "The Barber" Maglie. But he spoke of Willie Mays with genuine awe, in the same sort of tone he usually reserved for introducing us to Shakespeare or James Joyce. Mays was an artist, a master craftsman.

By the time I came along, though, the family was living on Long Island. The Polo Grounds was a far trek. Too far, and maybe too expensive. We were a family of five, and more than once during the 1950s my father took a second job to help make ends meet. Not a lot of time for trips to upper Manhattan.

So we talked baseball a lot. We listened to games on radio and watched them on our small black-and-white TV. And we devoured the sports pages of the *Daily News* that my father brought home each night from The City. Sometimes he'd take us into the street to play stickball. Sure, it was the tree-lined lanes of Levittown, but with an old broom handle and a new Spaldeen we felt like we were on 155th—and Willie might join us any minute.

We were heartbroken—my father, my brother Bill, and I—when the Giants left New York. Even my mother and sister understood. During the 1960s, we'd catch games on TV, taking confidence if we glimpsed the high-kick delivery of Juan Marichal, and dying at season's end as—too often—the Giants would fall short.

I never took my father to Candlestick. I moved here in the early 1970s with my own family and began to build a life. Not long after, my father retired. My folks had never been ones to travel much, but they came west a number of times, once for a long-dreamed-of tour of the coast. ("You know,

your mother and I have never seen Yosemite. Or San Simeon . . . they say that's really something.") Other visits were shorter and family centered: my nephew's graduation from Santa Clara, my son's graduation from Santa Cruz. A trip to Candlestick just never fit the schedule.

So my father and I talked baseball over the phone. He'd ask had I been to any games and how was the team doing. ("There was a Bonds who played for them years back—is this kid Barry related?") And he'd weigh in with reports from the New York scene. ("Did you hear the latest out of this fella Steinbrenner? Jeez, is he something?")

He knew the horror stories of Candlestick wind and had heard me describe frigid night games. Maybe just as well we never took in the 'Stick. He also heard the hope in my voice each time an attempt for a new ballpark rose up, only to die in the dust.

That all changed with the coming of Pac Bell. *The Giants did it,* I told him. They were going to build a new park right on the waterfront. Dad had been here during the war, before shipping out to the Philippines, and could even picture the spot.

I fed him constant updates. I went to the groundbreaking and gave him a complete report, telling him how Willie had cried to learn the street would bear his name. I sent photos back to New York. I videotaped the construction in progress and sent him the tape as a birthday present. And even though he balked now at the thought of travel, I nursed a secret fantasy that I'd fly him out for Opening Day.

The day the Giants closed the door at Candlestick, Dad was in the hospital. The message from my brother two days before had been calm: "He's feeling a little dizzy. We'll keep you posted." Eight days later, he was dead, and I was caught in the Philadelphia airport, waiting for my connection so I could join my sister and brother at his side.

I'll never get to take my dad to Pac Bell Park. Maybe I knew I never would. But I don't think I need to. He's right here with me, and we're watching sailboats slice along the Cove. We're screaming in ecstasy as Marvin stretches a perfect bunt into a stand-up triple on a bad throw. He's just one seat over, taking in all the sights, sounds, and spirit of the ballpark we can finally share.

Well, Pop, what d'ya think? Isn't she something?

Rick Clogher is the editor of *Splash Hit!* and a longtime Bay Area editor and writer.

7 A Park for the Fan, a Team for the Community

IF PAC BELL PARK'S WILLIE MAYS PLAZA IS THE MOST MAJESTIC ENTRANCE IN baseball, the Marina Gate in Seals Plaza, at the opposite end of the diamond, is the most spectacular. It's the corner of the park that lets you know, without a doubt, that you're in San Francisco—and reminds you why you never want to leave.

Where else can a fan travel directly to a ballpark by boat? Just in time for the first pitch, ferries arrive from Marin County's Sausalito, Tiburon, and Larkspur Landing, and from Alameda, Richmond, and Oakland's Jack London Square in the East Bay, carrying hundreds of excited passengers for whom the party has already begun. The view from the gate ranks as the prettiest in baseball: palm trees wave above the entrance; rows of graceful sailboats nestle in the marina, their stark white sails vivid against the dark blue water; and the gray-green Oakland hills mark the eastern horizon. It's got a warm Mediterranean feel, like a northern California Cote d'Azur.

The Giants knew the waterfront park would be beautiful, but nobody anticipated the popularity of McCovey Cove or the armada it would attract. They come in all shapes and sizes—sailboats, kayaks, catamarans, and outboards. And there are the one-of-a-kind craft: the retired presidential yacht *Potomac* visited one Saturday, and a replica of a nineteenth-century Tall Ship, its yellowed sails and ornate wooden masts visible above the right-field fence, came for a few games that same weekend. Giants broadcaster Jon Miller keeps a photo logbook at the ready to help distinguish the regulars from the newcomers, because on some days there are more boats in the Cove than fans watching the game from the Portwalk. Coast Guard and police boats patrol to keep the peace, but they have little to do thanks to the good cheer that prevails in the hardball fleet.

After every Sunday game, the kids get to take over Pac Bell Park. Families get to share a special moment, and some future Hall of Famer may get his first taste of the majors.

It's a dog-day afternoon in McCovey Cove, as Justy, Kyma, Rio, Shadow, Surfer, and Topper—better known as the Baseball Aquatic Retrieval Korps—patrol the waters, diving after any ball that hits the Bay. Bark if you're a Giants fan.

Giants fans turn McCovey Cove into a bayside booster club for the home team: canoes get new paint jobs, and one die-hard shows that the ballpark doesn't have a monopoly on giant gloves.

Tom Hoynes of Alameda is perhaps the most famous—and most frequent—sailor of the Cove. He attended every home game of the inaugural season in his ten-foot Zodiac, listening to the play-by-play on the radio. Hoynes nabbed four of the Giants' six official Splash Hits. (All six were hit by Barry Bonds; opposing players hit only two.) Hoynes also fished out hundreds of batting-practice homers. He accumulated so many BP homers in the first month or so of the season that he decided to spread a little joy. He soon began giving them away to kids on the Portwalk.

There's one other homer that he didn't keep. In early September, when the San Diego Padres' John Mabry hit one into the Cove on a bounce off the Portwalk, Hoynes threw it back to fans on the Arcade, so they could give it the traditional treatment for a home run ball hit by an opponent: they tossed it back into the park.

On Saturdays, the Giants keep a portion of the Cove clear for the most singular feature of this singular ballpark: the Baseball Aquatic Retrieval Korps (yes, BARK)—Portuguese water dogs trained to retrieve Splash Hits. Local comic Don Novello—best known as his alter ego, Father Guido Sarducci—first brought the idea to the Giants in 1996 after they got the go-ahead to build Pac Bell. Most people thought the suggestion was a joke, but team officials think it strikes the right note of San Francisco irreverence.

"I went all over the country talking about Pac Bell and the question I heard most was, 'Are you really going to have dogs go after home-run balls in the Bay?'" Larry Baer recalls with a chuckle. The Giants teamed up with Pets in Need—a Redwood City animal shelter—and a local club devoted to Portuguese water dogs, a hardy breed with a long history of working with fishermen.

"It's the only park around where they can have a seventh-inning fetch."
—Dodgers broadcaster Vin Scully, commenting on Father Guido Sarducci's BARK

The BARK members—Rio, Justy, Kyma, Shadow, Surfer, and Topper—were an immediate sensation with fans, who cheered them as they jumped off the good ship *Jollipup* during batting practice to retrieve homers (the paucity of official Splash Hits meant the dogs had little actual work during games). Now, on Saturdays, it's sometimes impossible to remember how it used to be around here: this was an anonymous, rarely used boat channel surrounded by crumbling warehouses. The park, the fans, the ferries, the dogs, and Cove regulars like Tom Hoynes, Joe Figone, and Steve Jackson have turned it into an only-in-San Francisco waterfront carnival—with a baseball game in the center ring.

Just as Pac Bell turned a forlorn stretch of San Francisco Bay into cheerful McCovey Cove, it has helped turn the South Beach/China Basin area into a thriving neighborhood that draws tourists and visitors as well as new residents who suddenly want to live near the ballpark. The old warehouse district was, to be sure, already showing signs of revival thanks to the dot-com boom. But Pac Bell Park has given it a throbbing, vital pulse. It's hard to believe, but some of the team's best neighborhood fans once were detractors who were opposed to siting the stadium here.

In fact, the opposition of local residents and businesspeople defeated an earlier attempt at building a stadium nearby. So when Proposition B landed on the ballot in 1996, the Giants went all out to win the support of their future neighbors. Team officials walked the streets, block by block, building by building, like politicians running for office. There were some 271 public hearings and countless more local meetings. The team even flew a group of skeptical locals to Denver's LoDo district to see how Coors Field had enlivened that neighborhood.

Early on, the Giants formed a partnership with one influential neighbor: Delancey Street, the legendary rehabilitation program for addicts and former convicts, which has its business

Fans in the Arcade are so close that they're a part of the action. Here, loyal Giants fans toss back a rare right-field home run hit by an opponent.

A Park for the Fan

headquarters and residence complex just blocks away on the Embarcadero. "We figured a struggling baseball team and a halfway house have a lot in common," Larry Baer jokes. Delancey Street founder Mimi Silbert quickly became one of the team's best allies, lobbying on its behalf before countless community hearings (Delancey Street, in turn, became the team's official movers).

"When the sun's going down, you can see the reflection of the light on some of the windows up in the Berkeley and Oakland hills, and it looks like little campfires. It's magnificent." —Mike Krukow, Giants broadcaster and former Giants pitcher

The club found other ways to be a good neighbor: it worked with state coastal officials to create pleasing public access—the beautiful Portwalk—where there had never been a walkway. It reassured residents that the stadium wouldn't dwarf everything, like a downtown Candlestick Park, and guaranteed that by setting the building far back from the street. The team also went along with a liquor license moratorium, to ensure that the residential neighborhood wouldn't become a nightclub district. Now, although local bars and restaurants do a hopping business—from Zeke's, a popular old

It may look like the South of France (opposite), but it's South Beach, and Giants fans reach their favorite "resort" by boat, car, bus, and light rail.

sports bar on Third and Brannan, to the string of trendy new spots on Second that includes Infusion, the Twenty-First Amendment, Maya, Paragon, and MoMos—the neighborhood isn't dominated by bars and their rowdy clientele the way other ballpark districts are.

Perhaps most important, the Giants worked aggressively with transit officials to make sure that dire warnings about traffic and parking nightmares didn't come true. More than half of all fans

"You always want to try and improve on what people think is the best. Well, this place is probably the best right now."

—Dave Howard, New York Mets' senior vice president for business and legal affairs, on Pac Bell Park and his team's hopes for a new ballpark

now take public transit; many more simply walk from downtown or the surrounding area. And while the limited number of parking spaces in the Giants' plans alarmed some locals—only five thousand designated spots—the worry proved pointless: an average of one thousand spaces went unused during every home game.

The team faced flak, too, over the Coca-Cola Fan Lot, which was built in exchange for Coke's contributions to the park. The Fan Lot features an eighty-foot-long Coke bottle that houses four slides, and early on some children's advocates warned against the imposition of such commercialism on kids. But the team swayed public opinion by promising to let children use the Fan Lot when the Giants are traveling—essentially creating a new playground for an underserved neighborhood with a growing population of kids. Another corner of the park, the new Catholic Hospital West facility on

So many people walk to Pac Bell that on game days some intersections look like the start of the Bay to Breakers; other fans just leave the work to MUNI.

SIMPLY THE BEST *by Peter Gammons*

IT CAN BE A NATIONAL ESPN or Fox Sports game, or a highlight on Airport-Vision or *CNN Headline News,* and you don't have to be told. You *know* it's the Giants and that it's San Francisco.

There is the Bay Bridge stretching to the horizon; or the view of the brick wall in right field and the dudes in wet suits on surfboards in McCovey Cove, in between the Morgan 4l and the Boston Whalers, the kayaks and the fishing boats. There's The Glove in left-center field, or a shot of the lines waiting at Orlando's Caribbean Barbecue for the jerk chicken and a Red Stripe, or maybe three kids with a father watching the glassed-in batting cages.

It is Pac Bell, it is Peter Magowan, it is the Giants. It is the best baseball park ever built, even if you don't like garlic fries. OK, this couldn't be done in Queens or Atlanta or Detroit because they aren't San Francisco, but that's the point. Pac Bell is The City, and it has brought out the baseball town in a market whose previous vision of baseball was a pitcher's hat blowing toward center field.

The worst seats in the house still give you a view of the Bay Bridge and the marina. As great as Camden Yards, Turner Field, The Jake, and Coors Field are, this is the best fan's ballpark because it was conceived, built, and paid for by Magowan, a legitimate baseball fan, and his investor group. In fact, when he put together the partnership to buy the Giants, Magowan was told that within a year he'd be upstairs in an owners' box to avoid the acid tongues of Bay Area fans. He hasn't moved yet from his seats right next to the dugout, and I'm betting he never will.

Pac Bell is unique, right down to the waterside knothole area, so fans outside the park can watch for free. It also has the smallest foul territory in the majors and that wacky right-field wall, which was inspired by the Hundred House walls at Groton School where Magowan played stickball growing up—walls, the story goes, that were conceived by Theodore Roosevelt and Frederick Law Olmstead.

And let's face it: Pac Bell is warmer than Candlestick because Magowan had the park built high behind home plate, where the winds whip from the southeast from May to September. On a night that touched forty-eight degrees with wind, you couldn't feel the cold air in the outfield seats.

San Francisco hardly needs a tourism boost, but Pac Bell has given it one, and it has provided proof of the city's baseball identity. For years, there was a core of 15,000 fans who would brave the tundra of Candlestick, but San Franciscans claimed there was a whole other world of fans here. And they were right. A provincial eastern baseball snob will find in three innings of wandering the park that these are some of the most sophisticated baseball fans in the country, and knowledgeable about a lot more than what happens in the Eastern Time Zone. "We've always known that there was a terrific baseball audience in this area," Magowan says.

The ballpark is also the first privately financed one since Dodger Stadium in 1962, a fact that makes Magowan none too popular with most of his fellow owners. As a whole, they want to be able to blackmail cities out of public funds and put schools in receivership (as they did in Cleveland for a football stadium). They want to rob the taxpayers, which is what happened in Maryland when they had to build two football stadiums—one for the Redskins, the other for the Ravens.

Magowan, instead, chose the high road, and a tough road it was. He was ridiculed by other owners and refused financing by hometown banks. He went through dozens of potential partners. But he kept plugging because the goal was worth it.

Where once there was nothing but empty rundown warehouses, in a city with no place to watch baseball, Pac Bell Park now rises between the skyline and the Bay with every home date a festival. For a fan, it may be the best park ever built. But then, it takes a fan to understand one.

Peter Gammons is a Major League Baseball correspondent for ESPN and a studio analyst on the network's *Baseball Tonight.* Three times named the National Sportswriter of the Year, he also writes a weekly column for the *Boston Globe* and has been a senior writer for *Sports Illustrated.* He is the author of *Beyond the Sixth Game.*

the Portwalk, near the Lefty O'Doul Bridge, provides a medical clinic for a section of the city that didn't have one. The clinic offers urgent-care treatment and community health screenings, as well as the latest in sports medicine.

"We started out not very popular, because people thought we were going to corporatize their quirky little neighborhood," Baer says. Instead, the team built a quirky little ballpark. Understandably, Baer's favorite compliment came from a local man who told him gratefully: "This park looks like it's been here for fifty years."

"Championship teams need to win with a true home-field advantage. We've been able to do that with the great support of the fans."
—Jeff Kent, Giants second baseman

The Giants franchise, of course, has been around for far more than fifty years, but in the past decade the organization has found new ways to be an active member of the larger community. With their "Until There's a Cure" day, the Giants became the first sports franchise to annually dedicate a game to AIDS awareness. And they continue to be among the most socially conscious teams in baseball, having added game events to benefit breast cancer education and treatment, prevent domestic violence, and reduce youth crime.

Individual players, too, get involved. Barry Bonds works hard, without much fanfare, to help the United Way on education issues, with special attention to the digital divide that holds back low-income and minority kids. Jeff Kent has raised hundreds of thousands of dollars on behalf of women's sports at UC Berkeley, with each of his home runs earning $1,100 in contributions from Kent, Webvan, and Macy's. And manager Dusty Baker works hard on military veterans' issues with the group Swords to Plowshares. In fact, every Giants player is expected to give back to the community under the team's "100 percent participation" policy. Most do more than the team expects.

There's another aspect of the organization that nobody talks about, but they should: the Giants have always been among the most diverse franchises in baseball, which makes sense in the multicultural Bay Area. The team aggressively recruited African-American and Latin players in the 1950s and 1960s, and its legendary teams of the 1960s were among the most colorful in baseball history, thanks to stars like Mays, McCovey, Cepeda, and Marichal, plus Jim Ray Hart, Bobby Bonds, Jose Pagan, Tito Fuentes, and the Alou brothers—Felipe, Matty, and Jesus. Today, while most teams have yet to hire their first black manager, the Giants are the only team to have had two: All-Star Frank Robinson (now a key advisor to the Commissioner of Baseball) and current skipper Dusty Baker, who has assembled a rainbow coalition of coaches and staff.

Opposite: Winner of the 2000 Willie McCovey Award, Ellis Burks proved an inspiration to fans and his teammates alike with his potent combination of stamina, flat-out hustle, and late-season heroics.

Robby Thompson shares a moment with his son as the Giants continue their pioneering "Until There's a Cure" efforts to promote AIDS awareness, and Marvin Benard and Dusty Baker know that building a community means that you include everyone, even wheelchair-bound kids who'll never run the bases.

In its best incarnations, the team has modeled an inclusiveness—rural and urban, veterans and rookies, batboys and batgirls and elderly "ball dudes," every race and class, even Portuguese water dogs—that is an example for the city and the nation. *E pluribus unum*, and then some; the whole is always greater than the sum of its parts.

The ballpark itself doesn't have to be greater than its parts; those parts are remarkable enough. From the statue of Willie Mays to spectacular McCovey Cove; from the clock towers honor-

"After decades in baseball's Siberia, the Giants have finally come in from the cold." —David Lassen, sports columnist for the *Ventura County Star*

ing Giants of the past to the Fan Lot for the players of the future—Pac Bell is without rival, the most beautiful park in baseball. Sometimes on a Saturday, if you watch fans arriving on ferries, hanging over the rails for a glimpse of the ball-chasing water dogs, gawking at the flotilla in the Cove, and waiting in line to slide down the Coke bottle, it's hard to believe anyone could pull themselves away to watch a baseball game. But they do, for every home game, filling the stadium to capacity and lining the Portwalk fence.

It's even harder to believe this park wasn't always here, thrilling the old fans and pulling in the new—and finally giving San Francisco the ballpark and the team it has always deserved.

8 The Never-Ending Story
by RICK CLOGHER

IF THERE'S ONE THING BASEBALL HAS, IT'S CONTINUITY. SONS OF PLAYERS become players. Fans become the mothers and fathers, the grandmothers and grandfathers of fans. Spring training leads inevitably to the Fall Classic, and around again. There's less concern for the day to day; a greater fix on the long view. In baseball it's been that way for more than 130 years, and the Giants have been part of it for almost that long.

Continuity was key for the Giants in their first season at Pac Bell. The experts wrote them off before the season began. Most of the country paid attention only long enough to see their glorious new home and to see them begin miserably in it. By the end of June, with the team dead even in wins and losses, almost no one outside the Bay Area was watching.

But the Giants held the long view. Dusty Baker quietly showed his confidence in his players, starters, and subs alike, and they paid him back: offense and defense that made Kent the overwhelming MVP choice. A personal best in home runs and a second place in MVP balloting for Bonds. Walk-off homers from Benard and Rios. Clutch hits from Aurilia, Crespo, Davis, Murray. Defense from Mueller that should have won a Gold Glove, and from Snow that did. Back-to-back complete game shutouts from Hernandez. Six straight wins in August from Ortiz. A pitching staff with the game's best home ERA. An almost unhittable bullpen. A starting outfield that committed only one error at home. And a year from Burks that inspired everyone around him.

The team tore through the last three months of the season at a blistering .686 pace, setting franchise marks for home runs and home attendance.

So while the experts looked elsewhere, the Giants simply compiled the best record in baseball. While more than a hundred players entered the free-agent shuffle at season's end, the

Bobby Estalella lifts Robb Nen high to celebrate the clinching of the Western Division title.

"Early in the year, the crowd, like the team, was trying to find itself. People were in awe of the stadium and were not as vocal. . . . By the end, it was great." —Giants first baseman J. T. Snow

Below: J. T. Snow provided one of the most dramatic moments of the year with his ninth-inning home run to tie Game Two of the divisional playoffs. Opposite: Jeff Kent fielded solidly, spoke softly, and carried a big stick. The most productive second baseman in seventy-five years, he was a natural choice for Most Valuable Player. Overleaf: Images of the division clincher, including an acrobatic Armando Rios, and the last regular-season sellout.

Giants had already signed potential free agents like Rueter and Nen before the stretch run. And while six teams quickly ousted their managers in October, the Giants ensured that Dusty Baker—named Manager of the Year for a record third time by almost unanimous choice—would stay in San Francisco.

Best of all, they got to experience October baseball in their very first year in their new ballpark. And despite the team's falling short against the Mets—including heartbreaking extra-inning contests for the ages—Baker viewed the future as even brighter: "We're a very good unit. We work well together as an organization, top to bottom. It takes a long time to build this sort of team. They're gentlemen. They're warriors."

It's somehow fitting that Pac Bell Park should host such warriors, such big fellows. Their new home recalls the great ballparks of old, and the Giants have captured some of that bygone era's magic: team loyalty and a mutual respect among players, manager, and owner.

Put those qualities into action and you build a team whose story lasts long beyond any single October.

TODAY'S ATTENDANCE

40,930

81st STRAIGHT SELLOUT AT PACIFIC BELL PARK
THE GIANTS THANK YOU.

IC BELL PARK

Bill Mueller covered the hot corner for the Giants like an asbestos blanket, with only nine errors on the season. Opposite: At the plate, Marvin Benard posed a constant threat to bunt for a hit; in the outfield he was near-perfect, committing just a single error all year.

Opposite: Livan Hernandez beams after defeating the Marlins on August 23, his second consecutive complete-game shutout, after blanking the Braves the previous Friday. Six-year-old Christopher Burks shows why it's good to have connections: The Giants used nearly a dozen family members as batboys and batgirls, and they got the best seats in the house. Overleaf: A jewel in the night.

FAMILY HEIRLOOMS *by Joan Ryan*

WE PASS THROUGH the turnstiles at the Lefty O'Doul Gate, climb a flight of concrete steps, and we're there. Section 107, Lower Box, first-base side. Our four seats are in the middle of the row, canted slightly toward home plate. Though situated brilliantly near the entrance, the beer stand, and the ladies room, the seats are as ordinary as the next guy's.

But to me they look like the cut-glass cake plate we always use on birthdays, and the Christmas ornaments wrapped in yellow newspaper, and the sequence of photos taken by the front door on the first day of school each year—all artifacts that tell our family's stories the way chips of pottery and remnants of stone walls tell the stories of ancient civilizations.

That's why we bought charter seats at Pac Bell Park. For the stories.

My husband and I envision our ten-year-old son as a grown man with children of his own. We imagine him sitting in the same seats in which he spent his childhood, looking out onto the unchanging geometry of the field, to the flags in center field, to the masts of sailboats beyond the right-field wall, to the great old glove in left.

We imagine him telling his children about the very first Opening Day so many years before. He'll recall how we always brought two containers of chicken wings and a bag of peanuts to eat during the game, and how, when he bought his fifth-inning *churro,* he'd savor it by taking bites only when Giants players reached base.

I can hear him telling his children that he fell in love with baseball in those seats during the Giants' first season at the ballpark. That's when he began to notice the little things: how first baseman J. T. Snow tapped his glove to the ground before

every pitch, leaning slightly forward, ready to pounce at the crack of the bat; how opposing outfielders shifted wildly to the right whenever Barry Bonds came up to the plate; how the clock, despite its prominence there in center field, never mattered at the ballpark.

I think of our seats, twenty-seven rows up from first base, as timeless, too. They're one of the threads that will loop from my husband and me to our son and then, we hope, to his children, tying generations of our family not only to each other but to a city and a team and a beautiful park whose history will become our own.

Joan Ryan covered sports for thirteen years before moving on to a general column in the *San Francisco Chronicle.* She has adjusted well to watching games from the stands instead of the press box.

All of us are created equal—

      some of us grow up to be Giants.